P9-EIF-097

God, I've Got a Problem

Ben Ferguson

Vision House

A SUBSIDIARY OF THE BENSON COMPANY
365 Great Circle Road/Nashville Tennessee 37228

ACKNOWLEDGMENTS

Scripture quotations, unless otherwise indicated are taken from the New American Standard Bible, and New Testament, 1960, 1962, 1963, 1968, 1971 the Lockman Foundation.

Quotations from the following are printed by the kind permission of the publishers:

Man's Problems/God's Answers by Dwight Pentecost, © 1971, Moody Press, Moody Bible Institute of Chicago.

3000 Illustrations for Christian Science by Walter B. Knight, © 1947, Eerdmans Publishing Co., Grand Rapids, Mich.

The Psychology of Jesus and Mental Health by Raymond Cramer, © 1959, Zondervan Publishing House, Grand Rapids, Mich.

DEAR ABBY column, © 1969, Chicago Tribune New York News Syndicate.

GOD, I'VE GOT A PROBLEM
Nashville, Tennessee 37228
Library of Congress Catalog Card Number 74-80778
ISBN-0-88449-007-6

Printed in the United States of America

TABLE OF CONTENTS

PREFACE

Most Christians face the same problems non-Christians face. However, many Christians are unaware that God has provided principles in His Word to help handle life's pressures and problems.

The purpose of this volume is to examine some of man's basic problems in light of God's Word. I am aware that simplistic answers do not solve the sticky problems of everyday life. However, I want to offer some Scriptural principles that hopefully will help us deal effectively with out problems.

We know that no single problem stands alone. Usually it is interrelated with others. Because of this, there may appear to be some overlapping in the treatment of these problems.

I pray that as you read this book God will enable you to grow in grace as you deal with life's problems.

Ben Ferguson

CHAPTER 1

———◆———

"GOD . . . I'M DEPRESSED"

Legend has it that an old man carrying a heavy bundle of sticks sank down by the roadside with a groan and wished he were dead. To his surprise, Death appeared and asked him what he wanted. "My bundle on my back and my feet once more on the road," said the old man quickly.

Life's roadway has many obstacles and dangers. One of the greatest of these is the ditch of depression that runs alongside. It's easy for burdens to trip us into this ditch, and having fallen in, we often wander around helplessly trying to get out.

Webster defines depression as being pressed down, gloomy, dejected, sad, to have low spirits. He also says, "Psychological depression is an emotional condition characterized by discouragement and the feeling of inadequacy."

Some symptons of depression are a collapse of self-esteem, the feeling that no loves or cares, a dwindling of interest in others, and an intense absorption in self. He also suffers from self depreciation—"I just can't seem to do anything right." Some depression is physical

1

which can be caused by physical exhaustion or an imbalance in one's physiological system.

Middle age, or the age of the "four-Bs"—baldness, bifocals, bridges, and bulges—is an especially difficult stage in a man's life. He feels he has lost his virility and often becomes depressed.

Depression may be caused by disappointment and the inability to live up to one's expectations. Peter stoutly maintained he would remain faithful to the Lord though all others deny Him. When the pressure mounted, Peter denied the Lord, and when the rooster reminded him of his failure, he went out and wept bitterly. According to some psychologists, crying is a symptom of depression, especially in men.

Depression can also be caused by success. Someone said, "There is nothing more disillusioning than having arrived!" Success, therefore, is not a shield against depression, but often the doorway to anxiety and sadness. The moment we become successful, we are vulnerable. Perky Cox, a socialite in San Francisco, knew nothing but success from early childhood. Yet depression stalked her until the day she escaped her gloom by leaping off the Golden Gate Bridge.

Depression is devastating because it cripples a person's life and draws him into his own tiny world of introspection. Such a person becomes wrapped in a cloak of self-pity and is useless to himself, God, and society. Self-pity and gloom can sometimes become so intense that one may see death as the only way out.

Because depression is demoralizing, it's essential that we know how to deal with it. Let me make several preliminary observations. First, our home remedies are not effective. It's useless to whistle in the dark, smile, or ignore it in the hope it will go away. These attempts do not work. Nor does it do any good to engage in "operation bootstrap." There may be times when we are so emotionally low we can't reach our bootstraps! George Axelrod, a successful author, gave his remedy for depression. He said, "I read my 'Who's Who' listing. Then I say to myself, I can't be all that bad."

Secondly, we need to avoid oversimplification. Becoming a Christian will not automatically solve all our problems, because Christians also suffer from depression. Further, if depression is the result of a physical ailment, medical treatment is needed. And if it isn't physical, it may be deep enough to require the help of a professional psychologist.

But if we are Christians, we have something going for us. We have a new insight about ourselves and have experienced the undeserved love of God our Heavenly Father. Further, as we look at Scripture, we discover God has made it possible for us to deal realistically with our depression.

Perhaps the greatest example of depression in the Bible is the story of Elijah. He had been God's spokesman for over three years, faithfully calling the nation back to God. In a dramatic battle with the four hundred and fifty prophets of Baal on Mt. Carmel, Elijah proved conclusively he was God's servant. God also affirmed Elijah by answering his prayer to send rain to break the drought. But as he returned to Jezreel before Ahab's chariot, Jezebel sent a sharp message to Elijah. "By tomorrow at this time you will be dead. I will personally guarantee it." Frightened, forgetting everything God had done for him, Elijah ran eighty-five miles into the wilderness.

Chapter 19 of 1 Kings describes Elijah's dejection as he sat under a juniper bush in the wilderness. "It is enough! Now, O Lord, take my life; for I am not better than my fathers" (1 Kings 19:4). Elijah is at the depth of depression!

As we examine Elijah's situation, we discover four things to help us defeat depression. First: *Get away for a rest* (1 Kings 19:5–8). This is what Elijah did. After doing a mighty work for God and running a hundred and ten miles, he was physically exhausted. He had been so busy caring for the spiritual needs of the nation that he neglected his own. Exhausted, he fell asleep under the juniper bush and had to be awakened twice by an angel to eat. After a good rest and food, he got up and had enough strength to travel forty days and nights to Mount Horeb.

Things haven't changed much since Elijah's day. Many still grow weary from well-doing. What begins as a fun or joyful ministry often becomes a wearying grind. When this happens it does us good to get away for an unhindered period of rest. Often a good night's sleep away from a problem will do wonders for our mental attitude.

Second: *Get your frustrations off your chest* (1 Kings 19:9–10). After Elijah traveled the additional forty days, he came to the cave in Horeb. There the Lord came to him and said, "What are you doing here, Elijah?" In effect, God was saying, "Elijah, tell me what's bothering you."

And Elijah took this opportunity to pour out his frustrations. "Lord," he said, "they didn't appreciate a thing I did. Even when the drought was broken, they went against me. In fact, they are looking for me now to kill me. Furthermore, I am the only one left who is Your servant and it looks like I'm wasting my life. It's no use living any more. I may as well die and get it over with." In one exasperated moment, Elijah poured out the venom that was poisoning his soul. And without realizing it, he bequeathed us a workable pattern—get your frustrations out in the open and tell God what's eating you!

God *is* interested in the things that bother us. He understands our problem and, rather than condemn us, wants to help us overcome our infirmities.

If, however, you think it strange to tell God your problem, then tell an interested friend. Someone has said that a psychologist is someone you buy to listen to your problems. Most people find verbalizing their problem helps them discover the problem is not nearly as big as they thought it was. God knew this and encouraged Elijah to get his frustrations out in the open.

Third: *Get a fresh awareness of the personal presence of God* (1 Kings 19:11–12). Elijah felt forsaken by God as well as the nation. He began doubting the power and personal presence of God. As Elijah stood at the entrance of the cave, a tremendous wind came up, so strong it split rocks; but "the Lord was not in the wind." Then came an earthquake; but "but the Lord was not in the earthquake." After that, a raging fire; but "the Lord was not in the fire." In a few moments, Elijah had seen mighty demonstrations of the power of God, but God was not in them.

When these awesome manifestations ended, the Scripture says, "and after the fire a sound of gentle blowing." After everything quieted down, Elijah became qware that God was in the gentle stillness. "And it came about, when Elijah heard it, that he wrapped his face in his mantle. . . ." He knew God was present; he wasn't alone; God hadn't forsaken him. In a moment Elijah received a fresh awareness of the personal presence and power of God.

When depressed, we, too, need a fresh awareness of the personal presence and power of God in our lives. When we are rejected by friends, it's easy to fall into depths of depression and insulate ourselves from God in our blanket of self-pity. We want God to demonstrate His mighty power so we can be aware of His presence. Instead, we need to seek God's presence in solitude and quietness because it is here the Lord will meet us with a fresh awareness of His personal presence.

Fourth: *Get back to work* (1 Kings 19:13–16). Elijah had been the instrument of God to begin a mighty revival in Israel on Mt. Carmel. But he gave it up and sat around moping about how badly he had been treated. God again came to Elijah and asked, "What are you doing here, Elijah?" And even after his rest and new awareness of God's presence, Elijah still complained about how mistreated he had been.

At this point God tells Elijah two important things. The first is to get up and get back to work! "Elijah, you were commissioned to be a prophet, so get up off your self-pity and be a prophet! Go and anoint three men. One of the three, Elisha, is to be your successor. As long as you sit here you will continue to nurse your self-pity." A return to an active ministry was necessary to get his mind off himself.

Then God tells Elijah: "You are not alone in the work of God. There are an additional seven thousand who remain faithful to Me." When Elijah learned he was not alone in serving God and that others were actively working with him, he overcame his depression and went back on the road to do the job God called him to.

Like Elijah, once we have rested and had a fresh awareness of the presence of God, we must get up off our self-pity and get back to work. Idle hands and minds provide fuel for depression, but resumption of activities takes our mind off our personal problems and makes us usefuland productive again.

Summary

All of us have times when we feel down, gloomy, dejected, and worthless. But God did not design us to be crippled by depression. You can defeat it if you will follow these steps:

1. Get away from the problem for a rest,
2. Get your frustrations off your chest—tell God about it,
3. Get a fresh awareness of the personal presence of God, and then
4. Get back to work.

Why not learn from the experience of Elijah? Do what he did and let God put your feet back on the road and your bundle on your back.

CHAPTER 2

"GOD . . . I'M TEMPTED"

A salesman in Longview, Texas, hunted in vain for a parking space and in desperation left his car in a no-parking zone with this note on the windshield: "I've circled this block ten times and I have an appointment to keep or lose my job. Forgive us our trespasses."

A police officer who read the note left this reply: "I've circled this block for twenty years. If I don't give you a ticket, I'll lose my job. Lead us not into temptation."

The police officer found (like we do) it's not necessary to go out in search of temptation. It finds us all too easily and quickly. Our problem is not how to get into temptation, but rather how to defeat temptation when it comes.

Temptation has been defined as "an effort to try to persuade, induce, entice—especially to something sensually pleasurable or immoral." It means "to arouse a desire." Basically, temptation is that inner voice that says "go ahead and do it" when you know you should not.

In order to gain some insight into defeating temptation, let us look at the experience of the only three perfect people who ever lived on earth. All three faced temptations. Two gave in

9

and lost their perfection. Only one was able to sucessfully defeat it. From the experiences of these three, we learn important lessons in how to overcome.

We see an illustration of temptation early in the Scriptures. Adam and Eve were given everything they could desire (Genesis 3:1-6). The only restriction was not to eat of one particular tree in Eden. Satan came to Eve disguised as a snake and said, "Go ahead, eat it. It won't hurt anything. God was selfish when He told you not to eat."

The crux of the temptation was not the fruit Eve ate, but the command of God. It was an attempt to get Eve to do what God said she should not do. She knew it was contrary to what God had commanded, but was persuaded to "go ahead anyway." The essence of any temptation is to get us to do what God has commanded we should not do.

It would be a misconception to say that temptations are ugly. On the contrary, they are usually most appealing. Eve found this to be so as she looked at the fruit of the tree and saw it was "good for food." Nothing wrong with the food value! Probably had plenty of every essential vitamin! Eve also saw it was a "delight to the eyes" and was "to be desired to make one wise." It represented a short cut to wisdom.

When Eve looked at the fruit, it seemed foolish to by-pass it just because God said to leave it alone. Anything so appealing couldn't be that bad! Perhaps God was just being unreasonable about the whole matter. Everything she saw and heard from the serpent provided her with the necessary rationalization to go contrary to the specific command of God.

While temptation appears attractive and provides the necessary rationale to do it, the thing it doesn't do is reveal the danger involved. Since that first human failure when Eve fell prey to the temptation and persuaded Adam to eat the fruit, human life has been filled with daily temptations. Unfortunately, our temptations are usually more than a desire to eat an extra potato chip! They strike three basic areas of life: physical, psychological, and religious.

The best way to see each of these is to look at the temptation of Jesus in the wilderness (Matthew 4:3-4). The first temptation Jesus faced was physical. He was hungry and Satan suggested He use His power to turn stones to bread and eat. "Use Your power to satisfy Your physical need for food," said Satan. "Why be hungry when You have the power to do something about it?"

And because we have become people attached to our creature comforts, we fall into the same trap. We are tempted to use our last dollar to get a gadget that will make us more comfortable. The tempter says, "Go ahead and get it. It will make life easier for you. God isn't interested in your material needs, so look out for yourself." To the youth he whispers, "Go ahead and enjoy sex before marriage. It's all right as long as you love each other." Physically the temptation is: "Why deny yourself things you want? Use everything and anything to satisfy your personal desires."

The second temptation was psychological (Matthew 4:5-7). Satan urged Jesus to throw Himself from the temple in order to make a dramatic show before the crowds below. What a scene it would have made! Everyone would have been astounded when Jesus landed unhurt.

Satan also tempts us to take premature steps in order to make ourselves look great. "Don't wait for God to promote you. He prefers you to be a nobody!" Have you ever had the urge to seek recognition by doing something spectacular? If so, you've experienced psychological temptation.

We also have religious temptations (Matthew 4:8-10). In Jesus' third temptation, Satan urged Him to make a "little" compromise so He could be a world ruler. "All you have to do is to fall down and worship me," suggested the tempter. "That's a small price for such a rich reward." The real issue here, of course, is who is going to be Lord of our lives. Satan says if we let him run the show, he'll pay handsome dividends. He says it's all right to bend the rules in order to get more for yourself. Compromise of your standards is the name of the game. If you've ever had the urge to hide your scruples in order to make a better deal, then you've had a religious temptation!

Satan chips away at little things in our lives and seeks to destroy our foundation by getting us to do things that seem insignificant. He bombards us with an inner voice which says, "Go ahead and do it; it really isn't all that bad. It's just a little white lie."

It's not easy to defeat the bombardment of temptation, because it comes in many disguises. But God gives us a formula to help defeat it.

First: *Recognize temptation for what it is.* Temptations do not come floating through the ventilating system—they have a tempter behind them! In Eden, the tempter came disguised as a snake and queried, "Indeed, has God said?" In our Lord's temptation, we read He was led by the Spirit into the wilderness to be "tempted of the devil." The "tempter" is identified as the devil and he, not God, is responsible for every temptation. It is categorically incorrect to say God tempts us. *All* temptations come from the devil!

Since temptations come from the devil, it is also incorrect to say that temptations come in order to strengthen our character. Though strengthening of character may result from withstanding temptations, that is not their purpose! The devil is not interested in strengthening our character. His aim is to cause the failure and destruction of our character. The Greek verb *peirazo* which is translated "tempted" means "to discover good or evil." It is his intent to discover weakness and defeat.

Because Satan wants to see failure, he strikes at our most vulnerable point. He repeatedly concentrates his efforts on our weakness until fellowship with God and harmony with ourselves is broken.

Wake up to the fact that temptations come from Satan, and he is not out for fun and games. He plays for keeps! Therefore the first step in defeating Satan and temptation is to recognize it for what it is—an attempt by Satan to get you to rebel against God.

Second: *Realize God has given us the power to resist temptation.* "No temptation has overtaken you but such as is common to man; and God is faithful, who will not allow you to be tempted beyond what you are able; but with the temptation will provide the way of escape also, that you may be able to endure it" (1 Corinthians 10:13).

Notice the verse says that no temptation is unique. Every temptation we face has been faced by others. As long as we think we are facing a unique problem, we're on the road to giving in and suffering defeat. Cheer up! Others have defeated your temptation; so can you!

Another delightful truth in this verse is that God will never permit any temptation too great for us. When Satan tempts us, he's operating under God's permissive will. God has laid the ground rules and Satan can go only so far. This was the case with Job. J. B. Phillips translates this portion, "But God can be trusted not to allow you to suffer any temptation beyond your powers of endurance. . . ." God knows exactly how much pressure we can bear. Before Satan pushes us to the limit of our ability to stand, God halts him. No temptation is too great for us, because God will not allow it to be.

A third truth revealed in this verse is that God gives us strength to defeat any particular temptation. With the temptation, God provides "a way to escape." This doesn't mean God halts the temptation. Rather, it means God makes it possible for us to break temptation's power. He does this so we can endure the temptation without failure.

When temptation weighs heavy, understand that God is vitally concerned and has provided you with the power to defeat your temptation. The power is available, but you must *want* to resist temptation in order to use the power that God makes available.

Third: *Use the Word of God.* When Jesus was pressed by Satan, He repeatedly turned to the Word of God. Each time Satan came with a suggestion, Jesus said, "It stands written," and then quoted what God had said. What we see here is the mind of God and the mind of Satan in conflict. When tempted, Jesus turned and quoted the mind of God in each matter. After Jesus used the Word of God three times in His defense, we read, "Then the devil left Him. . . ." The Word of God was used to defeat the suggestions of the devil.

While God Himself provides us with the external protection by limiting Satan's power, He also provides us with the tool for defeating him—His Word. The Psalmist cried, "Thy

Word have I treasured in my heart, that I may not sin against Thee" (Psalms 119:11).

The Word of God should be our standard of reference in all matters. When any suggestion goes contrary to the revealed mind of God, we should tell Satan what God has said about the matter. Never make the mistake of trying to reason with Satan. You may be smart, but no one is smart enough to outwit him. Allow God's Word to defeat him!

A word of practical exhortation: If you hope to use the Word of God as a defense against the subtle suggestions of the devil, it will require two things *First,* you must invest time in learning what the Word of God says. *Second,* after spending time learning the mind of God, be willing to obey His Word! It's useless to know what God says unless you have a willingness to put it into action when temptation comes. When you do obey, God will bring His Word to your mind and you will experience victory. However, when you choose not to obey, you will go down in spiritual defeat.

Summary

Ever since Adam and Eve, Satan has enticed man to go contrary to God. Because he frequently disguises himself as an angel of light (2 Corinthians 11:14), Satan often tricks people into following him because they believe he has been authorized by God. Do not be taken in by that lie!

You can defeat temptation if you will:

1. Recognize it for what it is—an

attempt to get you to rebel against God,

2. Realize God has given you the power to resist temptation,

3. Use the Word of God as your defense each time Satan comes and suggests a new rebellion.

I don't know what current temptation you may be facing, but God's promise is you can defeat it. Why not let Him prove it?

CHAPTER 3

"GOD . . . I FEEL GUILTY"

According to an ancient fable, the Greek poet Ibycus was on his way to Corinth for a music festival when he was attacked by two robbers. As he lay dying, he saw a flock of cranes flying overhead and called on them to avenge his death. The robbers nearby heard his cry but paid no attention.

All of Greece was shocked by the death of their beloved Ibycus and they demanded vengeance; but alas, no one had witnessed the crime.

A few days later in Corinth, at the music festival, the open theater was filled with a capacity crowd watching the performers impersonating Furies, the goddess of vengeance. No one knew it, but the murderers of Ibycus sat on the top row of the theater.

In solemn step the singers slowly advanced clad in black robes and carrying blazing torches. Their weird song of vengeance rose higher and higher until it paralyzed and chilled the blood and hearts of the audience.

At that moment, a flock of cranes swept across the sky and swooped low over the theater. From the top benches came a cry of terror, "Look, Comrade! Look! Yonder are the cranes of Ibycus!"

Every eye turned to the top benches. The murderers had exposed themselves by their guilty cry.

Most can identify with the two men who cried out their guilt. Which of us has not been surprised by our personal "cranes of Ibycus"?

Have you ever said, "I feel so guilty because I . . ."? Of course you have. We all face the problem of guilt.

Because we have a conscience, guilt is a problem. Conscience has been called "the voice of God within you . . . the knowing part of man which agrees with God's revelation of right and wrong." It was created in us by God to operate according to divine law. Since the testimony of conscience rests upon divine law, it's beyond our control.

The dictionary defines conscience as "a knowledge or feeling of right and wrong, with a compulsion to do right; of moral judgment that prohibits or opposes the violation of a previously recognized ethical principle." Human conscience is that inner awareness and feeling of responsibility for wrong action.

When the alternator light on the dash panel of my car glows, it tells me something is wrong with the electrical system and needs immediate attention. And every time we violate a basic principle of right and wrong, a little "conscience light" glows inside to tell us something is morally wrong and needs immediate attention. It's our early warning system that lets us know immediately when we have stepped out of bounds. Like the alternator light in the car, the light of conscience will continue to glow until the problem has been solved.

While conscience reminds us when we have done wrong, it is not sufficient to make us do right. The Bible tells us the condition of our conscience is determined by our conduct. We can have a "good conscience" (clear) by doing what is in harmony with God's standard. The writer to the Hebrews said, "Pray for us, for we are sure that we have a good conscience, desiring to conduct ourselves honorably in all things" (Hebrews 13:18). His good conscience was dependent upon honorable conduct.

When we do wrong, we have what Scripture calls a "defiled conscience." "Defiled" comes from an old Greek verb *mianine* meaning to dye with another color or to stain. Corrupt conduct "stains" our conscience, making us feel guilty. Paul told Titus, "To the pure, all things are pure; but to those who are defiled and unbelieving, nothing is pure, but both their mind and their conscience are defiled" (Titus 1:15).

When a man continues in error and corrupt living, he reaches the point where his conscience no longer responds to right and wrong. Paul says, "By means of the hypocrisy of liars seared in their own conscience as with a branding iron" (1 Timothy 4:2). When the hot iron of persistent wrong conduct is applied, one's conscience is seared and becomes desensitized to wrong. Ignoring the warning light of conscience will gradually reduce its effectiveness until it eventually ceases to function . . . the bulb or our "conscience light" burns out.

If you run a red light, and are like most, you immediately look to see if the police are coming. If not, you sigh inwardly and say, "I got away with it." But did you? On the surface it may appear that you didn't get caught. But just because no one saw you doesn't mean you got away with it. Your conscience will bring you to court and return the verdict—GUILTY!

Sin is the culprit in a guilty conscience. Paul says, "All have sinned and come short of the glory of God" (Romans 3:23 KJV). Man was created in the image of God and designed to be a reflector of His holiness. When man rebelled he was no longer able to live up to God's standard of holiness. Since then, whenever we do something that violates the holiness of God, our "conscience light" glows.

Few days go by that conscience doesn't inform us that we've violated God's standard of holiness. Unless we are able to deal with it, we will gather a load of unresolved guilt which in turn will cause many problems and prevent us from being the kind of free people God designed us to be.

The human is a delicate mechanism. Small problems can cause emotional, physical, and spiritual upsets. Of all the problems that plague people today, guilt is one of the most

pernicious and persistent. Dr. J. Dwight Pen-
ecost, a professor at Dallas Theological Seminary and an active pastor, said that the main
problem prompting people to come to him for
help is the problem of guilt.

What a handful of sand will do to a piece of
delicate machinery, unresolved guilt will do to
us—make a mess of our lives and constrict our
usefulness. Unresolved guilt causes emotional
tension and saps our happiness. True contentment and joy results only when there is no
inner conflict.

Several years ago, a young wife wrote the
following letter:

> Dear Abby:
> I have been married only two years
> and have already violated our mar-
> riage beyond forgiveness.
> My husband had to be away for
> six months, and during his absence
> I lived in our apartment. I was lonely,
> but everything went along fine until
> a month before his return. At this
> time I met a man, and his attentions
> led me to the most regrettable ex-
> perience of my life. I never thought
> it could happen to me, but I was
> unfaithful to my husband.
> Abby, my husband is the most
> wonderful man in the world, and I
> love him so very much. The guilt
> from this 'affair' is driving me out
> of my mind. I am trying to be the

most perfect wife possible to make
it up to him, but my conscience is
torturing me . . . Please tell me
what to do. And don't condemn me
for my actions. I've already condemned myself enough.
          —GUILTY AND ASHAMED

The guilt of adultery drove this woman to
the brink of despair. Because women are usually more tender and sensitive to wrong than
men, wrong conduct is apt to "torture" them
more. But man or woman, guilt robs us of
our happiness.

Guilt also demolishes our confidence, and
since confidence is based in part on conceal-
ment of our past failures, many people live in
constant fear that someone will find out about
their past. Like an escaped criminal, they
fear the discovery of skeletons in their closet.

Some years ago I read about Sir Arthur
Doyle's celebrated trick. He sent a telegram to
twelve prominent Englishmen with the warning: "ALL IS FOUND OUT—FLEE." With-
in twenty-four hours, all twelve fled the country. Why? They were stripped of their
confidence and feared something from their
past would be revealed.

Unresolved guilt can cause great emotional stress and physical problems. And to
escape the pressure of a guilty conscience
some drown their guilt in drink, while others
dull its sting by drugs. Others find a more
socially acceptable escape in food. I've heard

people say, "I felt so guilty for eating so much that I ate more to keep from feeling guilty."

Guilt may also drive a person to a life of reckless abandon in a frantic effort to escape the condemning finger of conscience. Many live at such a high pace they need tranquilizers for sleep and a roll of antacids to soothe the upset stomach.

Unresolved guilt will cause spiritual tensions, rob us of our fellowship with God, and make us afraid of Him. After Adam and Eve rebelled against God, they tried to hide from His presence because they didn't want to be confronted with their failure. Guilt deadens the desire for the Word of God and fellowship with other believers, because they serve only to aid conscience in accusing us.

Guilt will rob us of spiritual joy. We may go through the motions of being a "happy little soldier of Jesus," yet at the same time feel like there's a rock in the pit of our stomach. Going through the motions of Christianity with a guilty conscience compounds our misery.

David experienced the loss of joy when he committed adultery with Bathsheba and then had her husband killed. He poured out his heart to God in his great psalm of confession. "Restore to me the joy of Thy salvation, and sustain me with a willing spirit" (Psalms 51:12).

Sin had ripped away his joy, but once David experienced the forgiveness of God, he could rejoice and say, "How blessed is he whose transgression is forgiven, whose sin is covered" (Psalms 32:1).

Since guilt is basically a spiritual problem, it requires a spiritual solution. Human attempts to resolve guilt only magnify the problem.

Some of today's modern thinkers try to relieve guilt by excusing our actions. It's become popular to say we are the product of our environment; therefore, we have no reason to feel guilty. Some existential philosophers may proclaim our innocence for our sins; but the man in the street knows by experience he's responsible for his actions. If he were not responsible, guilt would not be the problem it is!

A popular cliché suggests: "Time heals all wounds." Time may heal all wounds except a wounded conscience!

Many years ago in Scotland, where sheep stealing was a capital offense, a farmer reported the loss of several of his flock. To catch the thief the authorities placed two officers on surveillance. Late one night they spotted a man approaching. Then just as he reached the spot where the officers were hiding, he turned and ran; but the officers caught him. He was subsequently brought to trial and condemned to hang. But the judge felt uneasy about the verdict and penalty, and visited the man prior to his hanging. After explaining why he had come, the judge asked, "Why did you run if you were innocent?"

The man broke down and sobbed, "Twenty years ago, I killed a man at that spot. I don't know why, but I feel compelled to return there often. But every time I near the spot, I break and run. My conscience has haunted me for two decades. I deserve to die. Maybe if I'm hanged, I'll find peace."

Time does not heal a wounded conscience.

Paying the penalty demanded by society will not heal the wounded conscience. A man may satisfy the demands of the State for a given crime, but that will not deliver him from the scourge of a condemning conscience.

If you have tried all the solutions and panaceas but are still plagued by guilt, perhaps you are ready for God's remedy.

Hebrews, chapter 10, has some practical helps for those who want to be freed from a guilty conscience. Actually, the solution on paper is easier than putting it into practice. Three things are necessary.

First: You must *accept that complete forgiveness is possible* through the death and resurrection of Jesus Christ. Hebrews reminds us the Israelites knew nothing of the complete forgiveness that is possible for us today.

> "For the Law, since it has only a shadow of the good things to come and not the very form of things, can never by the same sacrifices year by year, which they offer continually, make perfect those who draw near.
>
> Otherwise, would they not have ceased to be offered, because the worshipers, having once

been cleansed, would no longer have had consciousness of sins?

But in those sacrifices there is a reminder of sins year by year." (Hebrews 10:1-3).

Their sacrifices did not bring forgiveness, but rather served as an annual reminder that they were guilty before God. "But in these sacrifices there is a reminder of sins year by year." Israel was not permitted to forget that they were guilty of violating God's holiness. Each year as the High Priest entered the Holy of Holies on the Day of Atonement, they were reminded that the sacrifices covered their sins without bringing complete forgiveness.

But that system of reminders ended with the death of Jesus Christ. Jesus did not come to remind us of sin; He came to forgive! He offered Himself *once* as a sacrifice to take away the sin of this world. (All past sins, covered previously by animal sacrifices, were carried away by His death.)

"By this will we have been sanctified through the offering of the body of Jesus Christ once for all.

And every priest stands daily ministering and offering time after time the same sacrifices, which can never take away sins, but He, having offered one sacrifice for sins for all time sat down at the right hand of God" (Hebrews 10:10-12).

For by one offering He has perfected for all time those who are sanctified" (Hebrews 10:-14).

By His sacrifice, He made provision for the complete forgiveness of sins. The Bible declares that His death satisfied God, and the penalty for sin was paid in full. You can have complete forgiveness for every sin you have ever committed.

Second: You must *accept that God forgets when He forgives.*

> "AND THEIR SINS AND THEIR LAWLESS DEEDS I WILL REMEMBER NO MORE.
>
> Now where there is forgiveness of these things, there is no longer any offering for sin" (Hebrews 10:17-18).

How long do you remember a paid bill? Once we've paid the bill, we forget it. God says the death of Christ paid our bill for sin. Once it's paid He forgets it and never again reminds us of it!

Paul declared a new day for the believer: "Therefore let it be known to you, brethren, that through Him forgiveness of sins is proclaimed to you" (Acts 13:38). Christ bore the guilt of sin when He paid the penalty on the cross. Because Jesus Christ came to make us whole, He forgave and then forgot!

In practice, this means the death of Christ took care of all the sins we have committed before we trusted Him as Savior and Lord. It also means His death will take care of any sins we commit after trusting Christ. When we sin, we can experience instant forgiveness by confession. "If we confess our sins, He is faithful and righteous to forgive us our sins and to cleanse us from all unrighteousness" (1 John 1:9).

When you sin and then confess it to God, He forgives you. His forgiveness assures you He has forgotten and will *never* remember it again. Accept that fact!

Several years ago, I heard Dr. John Wesley White (as associate of Billy Graham) say that 95 percent of the mentally deranged people in England have rejected the forgiveness of God.

If God forgets our sins as soon as we confess them, why is it that we continue to be tormented by a guilty conscience? Any reminder of sins already confessed is from Satan. He is the one who causes people to say, "God couldn't forgive the horrible thing I did" and may prompt them to consider suicide. Once we accept God's forgiveness and believe He forgets when He forgives, we can stand tall and call Satan the liar he is when he suggests God couldn't or wouldn't forgive us.

Third: You must *accept yourself as God does.* Quit torturing yourself with a past sin like the woman who wrote to "Dear Abby." God had forgiven you and now accepts you as though you had never sinned.

You may say, "But you don't know the terrible thing I've done. I can't forgive myself." It doesn't matter how small or great your failing, God forgives and forgets. He took your sin and laid it on Jesus Christ. Now he accepts you in Him. For your own mental and spiritual health, forgive yourself, drop that load of guilt, and accept yourself as God does.

If after confessing your sin to God you pick up your bundle of guilt and take it home with you, you are worse off than before, because now you have rejected God's forgiveness and are carrying your guilt alone. Jesus invited us to come unto Him for rest. Part of that rest is rest from the torture of a guilty conscience. God has taken care of the problem, so quit torturing yourself. Accept yourself as God does, and you will have genuine peace of mind.

Summary

You can be free if you will:

1. Accept that complete forgiveness is possible,
2. Accept that God forgets when He forgives, and
3. Accept yourself as God does.

Go ahead; unload your guilt on Christ and enjoy the blessings of a clear conscience.

CHAPTER 4

"GOD . . . I'M BORED"

Have you ever wondered how different life would be if you could follow the wind and find yourself on a sandy South Sea island . . . riding the wild surf off Hawaii . . . sitting astride a camel by an Egyptian pyramid? But being in exotic places, doing exciting things, and hobnobbing with glamorous people is not part of our daily routine. The more we think about the excitement of travel, the more painful is the awareness that we're trapped by life's daily drag. Life isn't exciting—it's monotonous! The more our world closes in on us, the more frantically we seek to climb out of the rut by indulging in daydreams. But try as we might, we can't dream ourselves out of the rut.

Have you ever said, "I'm bored to death with the life I'm living; I never do anything or go anywhere that's exciting"?

Most of us have made this confidential confession to a trusted friend; but have you ever said to God, "God . . . I'm bored with my life"?

Boredom is one of the major problems infecting society today; all of us are susceptible!

Boredom is easier to describe than define. It's the weary feeling we experience around some-

31

thing or someone who is dull, uninteresting, or monotonous. It's the emotional fatigue stemming from the sameness of daily life. Boredom makes us feel life is little more than a rut (a rut has been called a grave with both ends kicked out!); the feeling of being trapped in a monotonous routine with nothing to look forward to but more of the same. It leaves us with an emotional flat tire.

Boredom results from our basic attitude toward life—the tendency to look at life as a monotonous drag. If a woman says she is bored with her lot, it doesn't mean she doesn't love her family; it means she is tired of seeing the same kids and dishes day after day.

Men often view their job as a monotonous bore. At the end of the day they come home emotionally flat with little desire to do more than sit in front of the TV, hoping to blot out the thought of going back to the "grind" the following day.

People become bored with their friends. After a while, they feel few of them have anything interesting to say. How many interesting friends do you have? If you are normal, the number will probably be under five.

Television producers are largely responsible for intensifying our boredom. Picture the harried housewife (wearing a frayed and bedraggled chenille bathrobe) standing at her ironing board with a mountain of unironed clothes; her children have made a shambles of the house; the sink is full of dirty dishes. In an effort to escape the chaos, she makes a mistake and turns on the TV. There a beautiful, shapely girl sways to the romantic strains of Hawaiian music. She looks back at the stack of ironing, the dirty dishes in the sink, the up-side-down house, the frayed bathrobe, and says to herself, "YUK!" (What she really feels like doing is kicking in the picture tube and running away!) Knowing she can't do that, she sits and seethes, feeling hopelessly trapped by the drudgery of her housework.

Dr. Isaac Frohman of Washington, D.C. was quoted in the *Enquirer*:

> "I would say that 60 to 75 percent of my housewife patients are stir crazy. After fifteen or twenty years of doing nothing but taking care of the children, dogs, catering to the husband, and doing housework, these women get sick. They get psychologically sick . . . a wife feels trapped at home. She is unhappy with her husband, bored with her children, and tired of the daily monotony.
>
> Compounding her misery is the itch of envy . . . resentment of her husband's exciting life out there in the big world of business. 'If only I could get out there and compete,' she thinks."

But men suffer the same type of boredom on their jobs. Some time ago, the Question Man for the *San Francisco Chronicle* asked a number of men on the streets of San Francisco if they were in a rut. (Notice how their answers reflect a treadmill quality.)

> "Yes, I am. I do the same thing day after day. Go to work. Come home. Eat. Go to bed.

Get up. Go to work. Come home. Eat. Go to bed. I got to make some changes."

"Yes, I am. I'm measuring all day long. Then I go home, sit down and watch TV. Next day I'm back to work, measuring again all day long."

"Yes, I work all day long and then at night, well, I'm a married man. I'm doing the same thing other married men do. I have a job in the day and I work on my marriage at night."

Dr. Roger Tredgold, a British specialist on psychological medicine, reported in *Parade*, "Labor management experts believe that too many workers regard their jobs as dead-end, dull, boring, and degrading!"

Boredom is not an occupational hazard, it's an attitude toward the occupation. In our impersonal mechanized society, every job has an element of the routine. But it's not the routine that leads to boredom; it's one's attitude toward the routine!

The housewife can look at her children as a trap or as a privilege granted to shape the lives of part of the next generation. A husband can see his job as a monotonous drag or as a small part of getting a significant job done. One's attitude makes the difference.

If not dealt with properly, boredom will cause emotional sickness. Some of the emotional symptoms of boredom are despair, depression, pessimism, and ultimately, suicide.

Dr. Frohman notes that bored women suffer from imagined ailments. To combat this, he prescribes they find an outlet—hobbies, sports, education—something interesting to take their minds away from the household. Such outlets may bring temporary relief, but fail to deal with the basic problem of attitude. An outing may do wonders for the moment, but once back in the house, the four walls of boredom close in again. And in a desperate attempt to break the drab drag, bored people may seek thrills in drugs, sex, alcohol, or the occult. In addition to the social impact of such fruitless efforts, the emotional toll and scars left on family members is immeasurable.

Some observers believe boredom is responsible for much of the violence in the world today. *Parade* Magazine's article on "Boredom and Violence" stated that countless surveys indicate job dissatisfaction plays a large role in the current national wave of discontent. "In seeking other outlets for their energy, more people are choosing violence and justifying it," Dr. Tredgold told the Royal Society of Health Congress.

It is easy to follow the warped logic of some who reason, "Why work in a boring job all day for a pittance when you can rob a bank and come home with a bundle?" The element of danger, even the threat of jail if caught, adds excitement and seems preferable to the dull routine of the job at the "sweat shop."

Boredom also creates spiritual problems. Many Christians blame God for their boredom. They feel God is too distant to be concerned about their problems. Some, because they know they have a room reserved in the "Heavenly

Hotel," adopt an attitude of living high till the "bye and bye."

Others bear their boredom as if it were a cross laid on them by God. They feel kicking over the traces would be "unspiritual," so suffer through life bored! Such an attitude increases the feeling of being trapped in a room without windows or doors. And not being able to knock down the walls, they grit their teeth and endure the daily boredom while glibly singing "Jesus is the joy of living."

Many try various escape routes which usually end up as deadend tunnels.

Some think a new job with more excitement is the way to go. (And changing jobs may bring a temporary respite.) But every job has its monotonous element.

Others seek escape in travel, thinking the excitement of being in a different place and meeting new people will banish their boredom. Travel may bring relief, but it is only temporary. Boredom will return.

Some think a higher standard of living would make life more interesting. So they secure a second job, put their wife to work, get a bigger house, a newer car, and higher payments. That kind of escape is leaping from the "frying pan into the fire" because it only gives you more comfortable surroundings for your misery. The higher standard of living makes you its slave. How ironic to work eighteen hours a day to pay for all the laborsaving devices!

It's interesting that Sweden has one of the

highest standards of living and also the highest suicide rate. Africa, on the other hand, has one of the lowest standards of living and the lowest suicide rate. A higher standard of living will not deliver us from boredom, because we can never buy our way our of boredom.

Face it! Most of our efforts only aggravate the problem; they are attempts to escape by running. One day we'll have to stop running, and when we do, boredom will strike again.

If we will stop long enough to take a good look at the problem, we will discover God has provided a way out. You say, "I sure hope so, because my home remedies aren't working; I'm tired of running."

The solution to boredom is not found in a constant change of circumstances, but in a change of attitude toward the circumstances.

The first step to curing boredom is: *Recognize that God's plan for your life does not include boredom.* This is a basic step. Many Christians see God as some sort of cosmic kill-joy floating around on a pink cloud looking for Christians who are happy. Once found, He takes immediate steps to make them miserable.

Jesus spoke pointedly to this when He said, ". . . I came that they might have life, and might have it abundantly" (John 10:10). Did Jesus say He came to make a life a drag? No! Christians convey this idea because they have a warped view of God. Jesus promised two things: Spiritual life in the "new birth" and life that was meaningful. Like any father,

God, our heavenly Father, wants us to experience a life that is full and meaningful with purpose and direction.

God reaches beyond our circumstances and meets the basic need. He doesn't promise us a new job with more excitement; a new place to live where neighbors are more friendly; a new mate who is more understanding; more money to buy things. These things will not solve the problem nor lift the pressure that squeezes the joy out of living.

God makes us new people with new views of life. When we trust Christ, He gives us new minds, new emotions, and new wills equipping us to see life from a different perspective. God gives new life, not new circumstances.

God's purpose in salvation is not to make us miserable; we do that to ourselves. He came to give life with meaning.

Second: *Realize that where you are is God's will.* Elijah is a good case in point. He came from obscurity to the courts of Ahab. Immediately God directed him to go hide by a stream in the desert (1 Kings 17). He spent months sitting by the brook *alone,* being fed by the birds. Think about it! Day after day, he had nothing to do except wait for the birds to bring his food and watch the stream dry up.

Nevertheless, Elijah, the "palace man," found joy and contentment in being alone in the desert without daily routines because he knew God had placed him there.

Our common everyday task is glorified when

it is in the will of God. The routine task, no matter how insignificant it seems, is God's will for your life at this moment; so ENJOY IT! Go ahead; enjoy it! Stop looking at it as a cross to be borne.

It may be that you are in a job you know is not God's will for you. If that's the case, you can never hope to be free from boredom until you find the job God has for you. Unless you have leading from God to the contrary, the job you now have is God's will for your life. When you realize your job is God's will for your life at the present, it will change your attitude toward your circumstances.

Then, ask yourself who are you working for? You might say, "I'm doing it for the man who signs my check," or "I'm keeping the house clean for my husband, but he doesn't appreciate it." No wonder you are bored; you are working for the wrong person. Too many go astray because they are working for the employer or mate rather than for God. It isn't the job you do, but for whom you do it that makes it worthwhile.

Paul gave some practical advice when he said, ". . . In all things obey those who are your masters on earth, not with external service, as those who merely please men, but with sincerity of heart, fearing the Lord. Whatever you do, do your work heartily, as for the Lord, rather than for men; knowing that from the Lord you will receive the reward of the inheritance" (Colossians 3:22–24).

The relative importance of your job in the eyes of men makes no difference, for you are not to work for their approval. It is to be for God, "It is the Lord Christ whom you serve" (Colossians 3:24).

When you wash dishes or mop the floors, it's for God. And when you feed cards into a punch press, it's also for God. All our work (whether large or small, exciting or routine) is for God, not man. If you seek God's approval, you don't have to worry about pleasing the boss. A simple realization of this should begin to alter your attitude toward your task in life.

When we murmur and complain about our job or station in life, we are doing it against God. If it's God's will for you to be a housewife, you will be judged by the kind of housewife you have been, not what you contributed to the local garden club. If it's God's will for you to be a mechanic, you will be judged on your merits as a mechanic, not what you could have done as a bank president.

Once you realize that where you are is God's will for your life, it will halt the search for happiness elsewhere; you know it can't be found anywhere else.

Third: *Personalize your work.* Much of our boredom results from feeling we are only part of the machinery. Impersonalization robs us of our sense of worth. Everything we do should be done for the person of Jesus Christ. Paul declared, ". . . whatever you do in word or deed, do all in the name of the Lord Jesus, giving thanks through Him to God the Father" (Colossians 3:17).

Would dishwashing seem easier if you were washing God's dishes? Housewife, that pile of dishes in the sink is "God's dishes" and He wants you to do them *for* Him. Thinking about standing at the sink doing "God's dishes" will give you a new view of a boring job. Once you realize you are doing God's work, it will add a personal touch of infinite worth to the task.

Finally, when you are doing a job, don't just involve your hands; put yourself into the work. Paul advises, ". . . do your work heartily, as for the Lord. . . ." (Colossians 3:23). Even lowly chores seem light when our hearts are in it. Such an attitude makes a world of difference between two people working side by side. One may be enduring the grind, while the other is enjoying his work. Why? One has his heart in the work, while the other involves only his hands.

How can you possibly put your heart into your job? Look at your job as a personal assignment from Christ, and it will take on new dimensions. Personalize your work in that way, and boredom will beat a hasty retreat.

Every day we walk along the brink of boredom and with little effort, can slip over the edge and be caught in boredom's quicksand. Escape comes not by struggling and changing circumstances, but by changing our attitude toward the circumstances!

Summary

God makes it possible to break the bonds of boredom when you:

1. Recognize boredom is not part of God's plan for your life,
2. Realize what you are doing is God's will for you, and
3. Personalize your work—do it as a favor for Christ.

When boredom rears its ugly head, send it down the road by applying these three basic principles.

CHAPTER 5

———————◆———————

"GOD . . . I'M LONELY"

Several years ago, a popular television series called Gilligan's Island dramatized one of society's gnawing problems. The series centered around the comical and usually frantic efforts of a group of castaways to extricate themselves from their small uncharted island. Between the emotional tides of high hopes and subsequent failures, they lived a relatively normal life. But with each failure, one sensed the group's despair. Life went on as they continually contrived ingenious ways of coping with their situation, and all the while hoping to contact the outside world. They frequently came close to freedom, but their efforts were always thwarted. It seemed they were condemned to live forever as marooned castaways on their lonely island.

I watched and laughed at the comical efforts of Gilligan and his gang; but inwardly, each episode struck a responsive and emotional chord. Most of us can identify with their plight because at times we all feel like castaways. Though we carry on our normal activities, we feel isolated from the rest of the world. At times it seems the whole world passes by our island of loneliness without seeing our frantic distress signals.

Like Gilligan and his friends, we desperately try to signal the world to stop and pick us up, but it passes by without slowing down or looking our way. After each unsuccessful attempt to break out of our isolation, we feel the chill damp fog of loneliness settle on our souls, and secretly cry our, "God . . . I'm lonely!"

Have you ever said to a friend, "I'm so lonely; I could just curl up and die"? In the quietness of our own souls, honesty impels us to admit we all suffer from loneliness. Because, like it or not we are as vulnerable to loneliness as the common cold.

Webster says loneliness is the feeling of "standing apart from others of its kind; isolated . . . unhappy at being alone; longing for friends, company. . . ."

Loneliness is that sense of solitude, gloom, and unfulfilled yearning for companionship. It makes us feel no one knows or cares about our plight. We feel isolated and cut off from the mainstream of human activity.

We could cope with loneliness if it were possible to pinpoint the *one* thing that causes it. But that's impossible because there are many causes of loneliness.

Death of a loved one can cause a once beautiful world to crumble and fall apart. My mother died exactly one week after my father. On the night of her death, her doctor called the family together in a small conference room at the hospital. "One of the saddest aspects of my practice," he said, "is to see one partner of a long, happy marriage die and the other left to spend the remaining years alone. The loneliness created by the death of one partner is almost more than the living partner can bear."

Loneliness can be caused by the feeling of being in the way—a common experience for many of our senior citizens. After years of productivity, they are tucked away in retirement homes . . . castaways from the "now" generation. Weeks and months can go by without any interest from their family. Loneliness closes in like a fog obscuring visions and hopes for any kind of future. Many feel they no longer have anything to contribute and would be better off dead.

Betrayal by a friend can also be devastating. Have you ever shared an intimate problem with a trusted friend only to have him break confidence? When this happens we begin to feel no one can be trusted and withdraw into our shell to nurse our hurts. We would rather suffer alone than dare open our heart to anyone again for fear of being hurt.

Society's "IBM approach" can cause loneliness. People in our mad, mad world have seemingly been robbed of their personhood. They have been made to feel like IBM cards stamped "do not fold, spindle, or mutilate." The vastness of our society makes us feel like numbers rather than people.

But the most profound sense of isolation is spiritual separation from God. Adam and

Eve knew perfect communion with God in Eden, but when they sinned, they were driven from God's presence and were the most alone, desolate people in history.

Modern man with all his technological know-how has designed equipment to put man on the moon and developed cures for polio, measles, and whooping cough. But with all our technical advances and sophisticated machinery, we have not been able to cure the problem of loneliness.

We were created by God with the need for fellowship and, unlike machines, were not made to sit in a quiet corner and run for days and years. We need to touch, hear, and rub shoulders with other humans. We feel alone and isolated when those we care about do not include us in their plans. The need to belong is part of our basic make up. We have to interact and relate to others to confirm our sense of personhood.

Things never satisfy! Assume it were within my power to give you every luxury your heart could desire . . . with one stipulation—that you live on an island . . . *alone.* You could have anything and everything you wanted—except human contact. How long do you think your happiness would last? Not long! Things do not satisfy that longing of the soul to see and be with other people. This is why placing a man in solitary confinement is such a terrible punishment; it violates his basic need to be with people.

Loneliness is recognized as a tragic characteristic of our frantic society. Lynn White, Jr., president of Mills College in Oakland affirmed, "The great disease of the Twentieth Century is loneliness. To use David Riesman's term, we are 'The Lonely Crowd'."

Dr. Karl Jung said, "Emptiness is the central neurosis of our time." The pressures and problems of our complex society have produced a world of lonely people jammed together like sardines in the can called "earth."

If it is any comfort, loneliness is not a problem unique to modern times. Many great men of the Bible spent time on the "island of loneliness." Think about Joshua, the conquering general and man who did great exploits for God. We read that after the death of Moses on Mt. Nebo, ". . . the Lord spoke to Joshua the son of Nun, Moses' servant, saying, Moses my servant is dead. . . ." (Joshua 1:1-2).

Imagine how Joshua must have felt when he heard of Moses' death. For forty years he had been number two in command as Moses' "Executive Officer." Certainly, he felt keenly the loss of a personal friend. But what struck Joshua was the overwhelming realization that the mantle of leadership had fallen on *his* shoulders. He was now number one in Israel. Moses, in his farewell address not long before, had already set Joshua apart as his successor (Deuteronomy 31). But now Joshua was alone. When a crisis arose, he could no longer say, "Moses, what do we do now?" The nation would look to him to solve their problems. The position of leadership set him apart . . . to stand alone.

The apostle Paul also suffered the anguish of loneliness. We usually think of him as a great preacher who almost singlehandedly shook the world as he preached the gospel of Christ. He endured many trials in the course of his successful ministry. But some of the last paragraphs penned while he was in prison reveal his lonely heart. He laments that no one stood with him in his defense (2 Timothy 4:16); he pleads for Timothy to come and see him because Demas had gone back to the world and others had been dispatched to points of ministry. The only person with him was Luke. We can sense the loneliness of Paul in his pleas: "Make every effort to come to me soon" (2 Timothy 4:9); ". . . pick up Mark and bring him with you. . . ." (2 Timothy 4:11). He needed the companionship of friends in his hour of trial.

These great men of God had moments when they felt like castaways and no one cared. But to curl up and let the world go by would be no solution. That would only compound the misery. Loneliness which is allowed to bud and blossom will eventually run riot and destroy a person.

But to break the smothering grip of loneliness is not easy. Most avenues of escape are deadends.

Some try the escape of popularity. A man may have world acclaim, be a box office attraction, and still be lonely. The suicide attempts of some of Hollywood's most popular "superstars" illustrate the inability of box office acclaim to meet the aching needs of the human spirit.

And paradoxically, we can't necessarily escape loneliness by being around people, for sometimes people accentuate our loneliness. We can be lonely at family gatherings and in a crowd.

Also, success is not a sufficient antidote to loneliness. Hemingway, an eminently successful author, said toward the end of his life that he ". . . lived in a vacuum as lonely as a radio tube when the batteries are dead and the current off."

Tennyson poignantly described his visit and assessment of the regal Queen Victoria when he said, "Up there in her glory and splendor, she was lonely."

Now add to loneliness the frustration of being unable to escape or cope with it . . . crippling despair sets in, often triggering suicidal thoughts. How tragic to be mired in despair so deep that death seems preferable to life.

Though human solutions fail to break our loneliness, we need not feel stranded; God has provided an escape from loneliness.

First: *Realize we are never alone.* God has given all who know Christ His personal presence. Only those who do not personally know Christ are truly alone!

When Joshua stood alone as the head of the

nation Israel, he experienced the loneliness of command. But God did not allow him to feel alone for long. God promised the nation success under the leadership of their new general, and more important was His personal assurance: ". . . as I have been with Moses, I will be with you; I will not fail you or forsake you" (Joshua 1:5); ". . . do not tremble or be dismayed, for the Lord your God is with you wherever you go" (Joshua 1:9). The promise of God's personal presence dispelled Joshua's awesome sense of isolation and inadequacy.

You may not be a Joshua, but God has a personal promise for you, too. Jesus told His frightened disciples as He faced the cross, "I will not leave you as orphans; I will come to you" (John 14:18).

After his crucifixion and just before His ascension, Jesus promised the disciples His personal presence: ". . . and lo, I am with you always, even to the end of the age" (Matthew 28:20).

Once we accept the reality of Christ's personal presence in our lives, we can face the pressures of daily living with the comfort that no matter what happens, we're not alone! Christ is present in our lives and we can talk to Him at any time. The woman who has to wash her dishes to the tune of three crying sick children and who has been housebound for a week desperately needs to remember that she is *not* alone.

Paul exemplifies this truth in 2 Timothy 4:17 when his friends faded into the woodwork after he was thrown into prison. With strong confidence he said, "But the Lord stood with me, and strengthened me. . . ."

We, too, who know Christ, have a friend who stands with us at all times and meets the longing of our heart for companionship. Read the letter of a nineteen year old who found this true.

"Two months ago I seriously planned to commit suicide by taking an overdose of drugs. My parents are divorced, and my friends have betrayed me many times with their gossip. For more than three years I have been smoking marijuana, and a year ago I started taking pills . . . Left alone in the house two months ago, I did almost everything imaginable to pass the time away. On the fifth night, I took some pills, started drinking, and playing sad music on the stereo . . . I dreaded the moment when the music would stop and leave me alone with myself. I lost track of time, but just as gravity pulls one to the earth, time pulled me toward death. At four in the morning I was sitting on the couch crying. I don't know why, but I picked up the Holy Bible and started reading it . . . An hour and twenty pages later I got down on my knees and begged the Lord to save me from myself. Now, sincerely believing in the existence of God and accepting Jesus as my Savior, I no longer feel alone . . ."

When we place our faith in Christ, we establish a *vertical* relationship with God that brings His presence down into our life.

After recognizing this vertical relationship

we need to: *Realize there are other people in the same boat.* Frequently we think we're the only lonely ones, but we're not! Elijah thought he was all alone as God's prophet, but he discovered God had an additional seven thousand people who worshipped Him. Multitudes suffer the same pangs of loneliness . . . the same desire for belonging and having someone who cares.

But to realize and understand is not enough; we need to reach out. It's amazing how we can overcome our own loneliness when we take the initiative and seek out other people who are down. Sitting around complaining about how lonely we are only adds fuel to the fires of our misery. Lee Truman said it nicely when he said, "The answer to loneliness is never found by an invitation brought on a silver platter."

Paul instructed Timothy to bring Mark along with him because Mark was "profitable" to him in the ministry (2 Timothy 4:11). The presence of Mark would be an encouragement to Paul.

Someone said, "People are lonely because they build walls instead of bridges." Because we are people, we need people. Helping someone else who is lonely will be the antidote to our loneliness.

As we seek to establish and nurture *horizontal* relationships, we begin to lift ourselves from the morass of our own loneliness and help others escape with us!

Finally: *Get involved in God's program.* It's essential for us to be engaged in the total plan of God for our lives. It's not enough to realize that God is personally present with us, nor that others are in the same boat. We must go on . . . reach out to others and personally commit ourselves to an active participation in God's program.

Paul reminds us that we are "partners together with God" (1 Corinthians 3:9). Think of it! You are in partnership with God in this life. As God's partner, you have a task to do; and you will not be completely free from loneliness unless you are engaged in that task.

Consider Paul's dilemma: He was in a Roman prison and couldn't go to Spain; he couldn't preach in the forum; he couldn't go anywhere. What could he do? He did the only thing he could do; he utilized his time studying. "When you come," he pleaded, "bring the books, especially the parchments" (2 Timothy 4:13). Paul didn't spend time sitting around feeling sorry for himself. He was busy studying for the day he would be released. He redeemed the time!

Did it ever occur to you that God may allow isolation to come so you will have time to do something you've been neglecting? Take a new look at your loneliness. Is God trying to tell you something you've failed to do for Him? Don't overlook this as a possibility.

Far too many Christians suffer from loneliness because they are *sitting* instead of *serving*. Loneliness comes when we sit instead of step out in the work of God. Once you begin to actively participate in God's program, you will find a deep comaraderie developing between you and the other workers of God. This will then place the *vertical* and *horizontal* relationships in proper balance. Final deliverance comes by realizing your proper place in the program of God along with other people.

Summary

Indeed, we all have times when we feel alone and deserted. But God does not intend for us to languish from loneliness; He provides an escape.

1. Realize you are never alone,
2. Realize there are other people in the same boat, and then
3. Get involved in God's program.

Why not follow the steps set forth above and join the freedom flight from the island of loneliness?

CHAPTER 6

"GOD . . . I'M BITTER"

During an interview at the big Naval Air Station in Lemoore, California, the Chief of Navy Chaplains said, ". . . most of our problems are human problems." This simple statement hits the nail squarely on the head. *People* are the cause of most of our problems!

Just think of it . . . if we no longer had people, prejudice would be erased; wars would cease; pollution and overpopulation would no longer be problems.

Let's face it, our humanness causes most of our problems. We are bundles of potential problems looking for a place to happen.

One of the deep problems of human life is bitterness. In his letter to the Ephesian believers, Paul addresses himself to this problem. He deals with the "gut" issues of unity, theft, lying, malice, and to "put off the old man and put on the new man" (Ephesians 4:22–24).

Then as the fourth chapter of Ephesians closes, Paul zeroes in on the thorny problem of bitterness.

As we examine the context of these verses concerning bitterness, we see that anger has a place in the life of the Christian. "BE AN-

GRY, AND *yet* DO NOT SIN. . . ." (Ephesians
4:26). God permits the believer to become
angry. But don't go overboard; anger is *permitted*, not commanded.

God permits us to become angry for several
reasons. First, anger is a natural emotion. The
inability to become angry would leave one
insensitive to wrong and make him apathetic
to the pressing problems around him. When
citizens fail to confront wrong with indigna-
tion and action, society teeters on the verge
of collapse.

Apathy has become a major problem in our
society and the church. Too often people put
on blinders and drive down the road of life
with little concern for righting wrongs. The
prevailing attitude is, "As long as it doesn't
affect my comfortable way of life directly, it's
none of my business."

A second reason for the permission of anger
is that it is expressed by God. Jesus Christ
became angry when He observed people defiling the temple by conducting corrupt money-
changing practices and selling maimed ani-
mals for sacrifice. If He has followed today's
political stratagems, He probably would have
suggested they gather for a summit conference
to work out a negotiated settlement mutually
satisfactory to all concerned! No chance! His
anger issued forth in corrective action. He
made a whip of cords, drove them out of the
temple, and overturned their tables.

Scripture declares that God is going to pour
out His wrath upon sin. The capacity to be-

come angry at sin and injustice reflects the moral *purity* of God.

A word of caution! Even though God permits anger, we are cautioned to "sin not." If we allow our anger to become personalized, it is a sin. Jesus was incensed with the defiling of the temple and vented His anger at the wrong. God loves the sinner but hates his sin. We know He loved those people because He went to the cross for them.

Though anger is permitted in the life of a Christian, such anger must be temporary. Paul also says, ". . . do not let the sun go down on your anger" (Ephesians 4:26b). Natural anger that is permitted to remain becomes a sin.

The Greek philosopher, Pythagoras, insisted that if, during the day, anger made any of his followers speak insultingly to each other, they were to shake hands, kiss, and be reconciled before the sun set.

In helping young people prepare for marriage, I always discuss what to do in the event of an argument. "But," comes the shocked reply, "we love each other; we won't fight."

Ah, the innocence of young love! I explain that as time passes, one of them will get angry and have a disagreement with harsh words. What do we do when harsh words come? Paul says, "Before going to sleep at night, kiss and make up." If you go to bed mad, you won't sleep well; and when you wake up, you'll be angrier than before you went to sleep. Failure to quickly resolve our anger nourishes it into a grudge, and some nursed grudges become irreconcilable, leaving us wide open to the devil. This is why Paul says, "And do not give the devil an opportunity" (Ephesians 4:27). Bitterness is a divisive tool used by Satan to drive a wedge between husband and wife and to destroy their home. Paul says, "Go ahead and get angry. But then settle the differences and forget it. Kiss and make up!"

Bitterness destroys friendships and the fellowship of churches. Notice the theme of Ephesians is the unity of the believers in fellowship in the Body of Christ. Bitterness will destroy this unity which is so essential in the assembly. The writer to the Hebrews sheds practical light on the subject when he says we are to follow after peace with all men (even those who have wronged us); "See that no one comes short of the grace of God; that no root of bitterness springing up cause trouble, and by it many be defiled." (Hebrews 12:14–15).

Have you ever noticed a bitter person can't keep his bitterness to himself? Misery loves company! He finds sadistic comfort in telling everyone who will listen how he has been mistreated. The result is (if allowed to persist) his bitterness will spread through the church like a malignancy. Barclay said, "There are reputations destroyed over teacups everyday."

A word of practical admonition: If you are unhappy in your church, you should either resolve your bitterness or else leave that assembly and find one where you will be happy. Failure to be reconciled will only spread your bitterness to others and cause them to sin.

Are you "burned up" with someone right now? Have you let your anger grow into a grudge or bitterness? If you have, here are three essential steps to help break the bondage of bitterness.

First: *Recognize it for what it is—a sin!* We are commanded to get rid of bitterness. Paul says, "Let all bitterness, and wrath, and anger, and clamor, and slander, be put away from you, along with all malice" (Ephesians 4:31). This command deals with a number of related disposition problems.

"Bitterness" (*pikria* in Greek) refers to a malignant disposition, a long-standing resentment, or a spirit that refuses to be reconciled. We normally think of it as holding a grudge.

"Wrath" (*thumos*), on the other hand, refers to the impulsive outburst—as when someone "blows his top."

During a ball game I once watched a player jump up, throw his helmet on the ground, and storm back to the huddle after the referees made what he considered a bad call. The announcer observed the player's anger and wondered out loud if he would seek revenge. Sure enough, the angry player tried to get revenge during the next play. His "anger" (*thumos*) gave way to "bitterness" (*pikria*).

The vehicle for expressing most bitterness (or wrath) is the tongue. A bitter person is frequently involved in what Paul calls "clamor," or loud talking. Most of us have noticed that loud talking or arguing almost always accompanies anger.

Another way we express bitterness with the tongue is through what Paul calls "slander" or "evil speaking and lying." It also means failing to tell the *whole* truth. Have you ever stretched the truth when recounting what someone did to you? If you have, you are guilty of expressing your bitterness through slander.

We are commanded from Scripture to get rid of problems that come from a malignant disposition. Paul says, "Let *all* . . . be put away from you along with all malice." We are to make a clean sweep of the bitterness that causes our dispositions to go sour. Therefore, if we hope to deal with bitterness, we must begin by recognizing bitterness for what it is —sin; and then deal with it as you would any other sin—confess it to God (1 John 1:9).

Second: *Try to keep from hurting others.* Paul says, "And be kind one to another, tenderhearted. . . ." (Ephesians 4:32). This is a direct command to display human kindness to other people. Kind (*chrestos*) means "pleasant or gracious." Greet people with a smile. A smile goes a long way toward removing seeds that would produce bitterness.

We are to be tenderhearted or compassionate. In practice we find it's easier to be compulsive than compassionate. A practical suggestion of how this works is to think of the damage your unkind actions might do in the life of someone else. Kindness and compassion accepts people just as they are (not as you want them to be) and a willingness to overlook personal hurts or wrongs suffered at the hands of others.

It's true many people are easily offended, but unless we are willing to display human compassion and kindness, we will alienate those to whom we are called to minister. It has been said the most flammable material in the world is the chip on the shoulder. Our conduct with others should be based on compassion for them in their desperate needs.

Jesus gave some practical instruction regarding the removal of bitterness in others. But people would like to blue pencil this advice out of the Bible! In His great Sermon on the Mount, He made it clear we have a definite responsibility to *take the initiative* in restoring those who hold a grudge. Notice what He says:

> "If therefore you are presenting your offering at the altar, and there remember that your brother has something against you, Leave your offering there before the altar, and go your way; first be reconciled to your brother, and then come and present your offering" (Matthew 5:23-24).

Jesus does not discuss who is to blame, nor whether the brother has a right to be angry with you. The *right* or *wrong* of his bitterness is not the issue. If your brother has something against you, you have the responsibility to take the initiative in restoring the brother and effecting a reconciliation. Failure to seek a reconciliation will hinder your worship. It's impossible to worship while you know a brother is holding a grudge against you.

In practicing human kindness, don't be concerned about who is right or wrong. The issue is reconciliation and restoration between two people in order to prevent the fruits of bitterness.

You might say, "That is a hard thing to do." I agree!

The hardest thing I ever had to do was ask forgiveness from a person who had no reason to be mad at me in the first place. If you ever to through such an experience, you will emerge with scars on your soul that will be a tender remembrance of God's forgiveness. Our rebellion broke God's heart and caused Him great personal heartache to bring us back to Himself. Nevertheless, He took the initiative to effect reconciliation.

Third: *Practice human forgiveness.* That's what Paul means when he says, ". . . forgiving each other, just as God in Christ also has forgiven you" (Ephesians 4:32b). We are to display human kindness toward those who are upset with us whether or not we have done anything to them. Forgiveness, on the other hand, is to be practiced with those who have hurt us.

The word "forgive" (*charizomai*) is a participle picturing continuous action. It means to forgive freely; not holding back or forgive grudgingly. Think of it! We are to practice forgiving *everything* others have done against us, whether they seek our forgiveness or not. We are to seek their forgiveness when we offend them and then go ahead and forgive others who offend us. That's revolutionary! We have the responsibility to be kind to them as well as forgive them, and in so doing, we will bid farewell to bitterness.

Forgiveness also involves a loss of memory. A failure to forget prevents full forgiveness.

One night two brothers were fighting just before bedtime. When their mother put them to bed, she said it wouldn't be good for them to go to sleep holding a grudge because Jesus might come during the night. Reluctantly one of the brothers agreed, "Okay, I'll forgive him; but if Jesus doesn't come tonight, I'm going to sock him in the nose in the morning!"

If we haven't forgotten it, we haven't really forgiven freely as commanded. God has forgotten all the wrongs we have confessed to Him, hasn't He? Then He has the right to tell us to do the same for others.

The divine standard of forgiveness is given to show the extent of full forgiveness. The standard is, ". . . just as God in Christ also has forgiven you."

Such a demand draws a number of weak objections. "But Paul, you don't have any idea what a dirty thing he did to me!" It isn't necessary to know individual circumstances. Think of the rebellious things we have done against God. We are to forgive "as God in Christ has also forgiven you."

We might object, "But that will be difficult.

It will hurt me deeply to forgive him for what he has done." Stop for a minute and think about how it hurt God to forgive us. It cost God the death of His blessed Son, Jesus Christ. It may wound our pride, but the hurt will never equal how much our sin hurt God. We are to forgive as God in Christ has also forgiven us.

Another weak objection we might offer is, "But what if he doesn't accept my forgiveness?" Whether or not he accepts our forgiveness is not our problem. We are to forgive and then leave it up to him to respond. God has provided forgiveness to the whole human race, but we know many will reject and trample it under foot. God knew that, yet He still holds out the "olive branch" of forgiveness to all men. God's forgiveness is offered whether we accept it or not; ours should be offered to others whether they accept it or not.

When others offend us, we are to practice forgiveness freely because without a forgiving spirit, we will never be able to pry loose from the grip of bitterness.

Summary

If you have allowed anger to develop into bitterness, you can break its grip by following God's pattern for freedom. You can be free from bitterness if you will:

1. Recognize bitterness for what it is —sin,
2. Try to keep from hurting others (display human kindness), and

3. Practice human forgiveness according to the divine standard.

Why not learn by experience the joy and release that comes from being liberated from the bondage of bitterness?

CHAPTER 7

"GOD . . . I'M WORRIED"

Children in Sunday School often sing a song that delivers a sledgehammer blow to our sophisticated adult world. With gusto and animation they shout:

> Why worry when you can pray,
> Trust Jesus, He'll be your stay.
> Don't be a doubting Thomas,
> Just take Him at His promise.
> Why worry, worry, worry, worry,
> When you can pray?

We listen to the children sing and are impressed with their bubbly enthusiasm, but don't respond to their advice. We might smile smugly and think, "They're just kids; they don't know what life is really like. After they've been knocked around by the world for a few years, we'll see if they can still sing their happy song."

We pat their heads patronizingly and mouth a meaningless "Wasn't that wonderful" and then continue putting more miles on our well-traveled "worry lane." Somehow, growing up turns us around and we hear the song as "Why pray when you can worry?"

Most children haven't been crunched by the machinery of an adult world. They usually have a refreshing worry-free world view. But years of hard knocks in the real world have a way of transforming the innocence of children into skepticism and trust into worry.

Worry has been defined as *anxiety*—a state of being uneasy or apprehensive about what may happen. The definition suggests a mental distress of agitation over some problem. Uneasiness of mind results from facing responsibilities or problems we feel incapable of handling. Washington Lyon once said, "Worry is the interest paid by those who borrow trouble."

In the New Testament, "worry" (*merimna*) comes from the Greek verb *merizo* which means "to divide." People who worry are "divided"—mentally torn apart.

Reading the newspapers exposes us to a multitude of problems capable of producing worry. Sometimes we feel we're sitting on a pile of gunpowder while world leaders play with matches.

Inflation is another problem to worry about. While we watch our money buy less and less, we wonder how to feed and clothe our families on a shrinking income.

Also, ecologists are giving more publicity to the energy crisis, and the word "rationing" is becoming a live option. For years we have lived with the feeling there was no bottom in the bucket of our natural resources; but now, faced with the possibility of shortages and rationing, anxiety begins to chip away at our peace of mind.

And in the midst of big crises are little daily crises: The garbage disposal breaks down; an important exam tomorrow; taxes due next week; our child breaks an arm; what to serve to dinner guests; what would be the "right thing" to wear to the party. When we add our personal crises to the national and international problems, we see why people are weighed down with worry.

Being a Christian doesn't provide immunity from the threat of worry. God doesn't provide a super anti-worry vaccine for the Christian. Joe Christian faces the same worry-producing problems that plague everyone else.

Once we allow pressures to worry us, they will snowball—the more we worry, the more we'll find to worry about. Someone once said, "I have lived a long life and seen lots of trouble, but most of it didn't happen."

Jesus placed His finger squarely on the main worries of life (food and clothing), "For this reason I say to you, do not be anxious for your life, as to what you shall eat, or what you shall drink; nor for your body, as to what you shall put on. Is not life more than food, and the body then clothing?" (Matthew 6:25). ("Anxious" is the same Greek word *merimna* translated "worry." In this sense, worry and anxiety are synonymous.)

Why do we worry? We worry because we fail to believe God. Jesus illustrated the point vividly by turning to nature:

"Look at the birds of the air, that they do not sow, neither do they reap, nor gather into barns; and yet your heavenly Father feeds them. Are you not worth much more than they?

And why are you anxious about clothing? Observe how the lilies of the field grow; they do not toil nor do they spin.

Yet I say to you that even Solomon in all his glory did not clothe himself like one of these" (Matthew 6:26, 28-29).

Since God feeds the birds of the air and clothes the flowers of the field, we can rest assured He will meet our needs also, for we are worth more than the birds and flowers. Jesus said that the Father knows what we need: ". . . for your heavenly Father knows that you need all these things" (Matthew 6:32).

Since God knows our needs, failure to trust Him to meet our basic needs is lack of faith. "But if God so arrays the grass of the field, which is alive today and tomorrow is thrown into the furnace, will He not much more do so for you, O men of little faith?" (Matthew 6:30). When anxiety creeps in, faith takes flight!

Failure to believe God is unbecoming to the Christian. Unbelievers don't know how to trust God for their "daily bread," so they worry. Jesus said, "For all these things the Gentiles eagerly seek" (Matthew 6:32). But God is not responsible for meeting the needs of the unbeliever (as He is for the Christian).

Christians have abundant promises from

God that He will meet their daily needs. ". . . My God shall supply all your needs. . . ." (Philippians 4:19). This is a promise! Worry about any need is a sin because it's a failure to believe God's promises. Nature shows how God takes care of the birds and flowers. We may see birds working, but we'll never see them worrying!

But you object, "If you knew the problems I face, you wouldn't call worry a sin." It's not necessary to know your individual problems because God has promised to supply *all* our needs. God has also promised to take better care of us than the birds, so why worry?

Worry will create many problems and won't accomplish a single constructive thing! It will only make bad matters worse. Several years ago, writing in the *Houston Times*, John Watson said:

> "What does anxiety do? It does not empty tomorrow of its sorrow; but it empties today of its strength. It does not make you escape evil; it makes you unfit to cope with it if it comes."

You can't solve any problem by worrying. Worry will not move you one inch in the direction of the solution. Jesus said, "And which of you by being anxious can add a single cubit to his life span?" (Matthew 6:27). When you worry, the problem seems to grow larger and larger by the moment. With just a little effort, worry can build your problem into a gigantic impossible situation.

Worry will create emotional problems making you tense, nervous, jumpy, withdrawn. It will impair your emotional ability to make decisions and make you progressively incapable of dealing with life. Every decision you face will become more and more difficult as you doubt your ability to make right decisions.

Worry will cause physical problems and chop years from your life expectancy. Dr. Alexis Carrel said, "People who don't know how to fight worry die young."

It will also add misery to the years you do live. Several years ago, Dr. W. C. Alvarez, the stomach specialist at the Mayo Clinic said:

> ". . . 80 percent of the stomach disorders that come to us are not organic, but functional. Wrong mental and spiritual attitudes throw functional disturbances into digestion. Most of our ills are caused by worry and fear, and it is my experience that faith is more important than food in the cure of stomach ulcers."

Worry will also produce spiritual problems for the Christian. Any time you do what God has forbidden, spiritual problems will arise, and since worry is forbidden, the person who worries can expect problems.

Worry will neutralize the effect of the Word of God in your life. In the parable of the soils, Jesus was talking about the productivity of the Word in lives. He underscored what worry will do when He said, "And the one on whom seed was sown among the thorns, this is the man who hears the Word, and the worry of the world, and the deceitfulness of riches choke the Word, and it becomes unfruitful" (Matthew 13:22).

You can read the Word, but if you are filled with worry, it will be unfruitful in your life. This explains in part why some never get to first base in their Christian life although exposed to the Word for years. They allow worry to neutralize the Word making it impossible to germinate and produce fruit.

Worry causes an imbalance in spiritual priorities. When Jesus visited the home of Mary and Martha, Mary was content to sit quietly listening while her sister "fussed about the kitchen" getting dinner ready. Luke 10:40 says, "But Martha was distracted with all her preparation. . . ."

In distress, Martha came to Jesus and complained that while she was working her fingers to the bone, Mary sat there doing nothing! "Lord, do you not care that my sister has left me to do all the serving alone? Then tell her to help me."

Jesus answered with tender reproof, ". . . Martha, Martha, you are worried and bothered about so many things; but only a few things are necessary, really only one: for Mary has chosen the good part, which shall not be taken away from her" (Luke 10:41–42). A modern paraphrase might read, "Martha, you're worried about putting on a big dinner when a sandwich would be fine. Mary has her priorities right. It's more important to hear the Word."

Worry will cause us to lose sight of the imminent return of the Lord, and allowing our minds to become enmeshed with daily cares and problems negates the urgency to be prepared for His coming. Jesus said, "Be on guard, that your hearts may not be weighted down with dissipation and drunkenness, and the worries of life, and so that day comes on you suddenly like a trap" (Luke 21:34).

Most of us know worry paves the road to misery! But knowledge without a remedy only intensifies that misery. Is there any way we can combat the problem of worry? If you have ever worried, God has good news for you; He has made it possible for you to stop worrying. Though God does not promise to remove the pressures that produce worry, He does make it possible for us to face the pressures of life with inner peace. God does not suggest that we follow His way to cure worry—He commands it! God's cure for worry involves three things:

First: *Stop worrying and start trusting.* Jesus said, "Do not be anxious then, saying 'what shall we eat?' or, 'what shall we drink?' or, 'with what shall we clothe ourselves?' For all these things the Gentiles eagerly seek; for your heavenly Father knows that you need all these things" (Matthew 6:31-32). The command to stop worrying is based on the Father's care. God takes care of the birds and flowers (and we are more precious in His sight), therefore, He will take care of us, too. Let God be God; He commands us to stop worrying about our daily needs.

We are also to start trusting God to meet our

needs. We have His written guarantee that He will meet all our needs. Jesus said quit worrying about things, and ". . . seek first His kingdom, and His righteousness; and all these things (physical necessities) shall be added to you" (Matthew 6:33). God has promised (in writing!) to meet our needs; so start trusting Him. Let Him be God; stop usurping His place as provider.

I have a health insurance policy which carefully details everything that is covered should I become ill. If anything is not covered, it says so. Once I know what the policy covers, I need no longer worry about the medical costs in that area. Likewise, the Bible contains a statement of all God has promised us. Since He has given us His "policy," we should trust Him to provide the promised benefits.

By contemporary standards my family was poor when I was growing up. My dad was a hard working farmer with almost nothing left over at the end of the year to provide the extras. But whenever I needed new shoes, lunch money, or a hair cut, I simply told my father, "I need . . ." and never worried about where the money was coming from; my father always took care of my needs. Conversely, God *our Father*, has promised to take care of all our needs; we have no need to worry.

Second: *Stop straining and turn loose.* Does that sound hard to do? If it does, it's because we think God is not interested in solving our problems. Did God care enough to take care of our sin problem on the cross? He did! Then doesn't it stand to reason if He was interested enough to give us *life*, He is interested in helping us with the problems of life?

"Casting all your anxiety upon Him, because he cares for you" (1 Peter 5:7). God *does* care for us. ". . . God demonstrates His own love toward us, in that while we were yet sinners, Christ died for us" (Romans 5:8). The cross is irrefutable proof that He cares and wants to bear out burdens.

What does "casting all your anxiety upon Him" mean? It means we are to give Him all our problems by simply letting go of them. He doesn't tell us to *throw* our cares on Him as the English seems to convey. The Greek word means to *hand* them to Him. If we had to throw them His way, it would imply He is distant, but God is closer to us than hands and feet.

Assume you were carrying a hundred pound weight on your shoulders. If I told you to throw it fifty feet, you would say, "That's impossible." I agree. But if I told you to quit straining and let it fall to the ground, it would be easy.

Once an old woman carried a huge bundle of sticks on her back as she walked down the road. A man in a truck stopped and offered her a ride. Gratefully she accepted and climbed in the back of the truck to join several other passengers. As the truck drove down the road, the woman kept the bundle of sticks on her back. When one of the passengers suggested she lay the bundle down, the old woman replied, "Oh no, I couldn't do that. It's enough that the man is carrying me. I wouldn't ask him to carry my bundle too."

1 Peter 5:7 is telling us to quit straining with our burdens, turn them loose and let them fall on Christ. That thought has been captured in a phrase of a song, "Take your burdens to the Lord and leave them there." We are invited to give our worries to the Lord so He can carry them for us. It's His responsibility, not ours.

Third: *Stop the panic and start praying.* This beautiful command is recorded in Paul's letter to the Philippian church.

> "Be anxious for nothing, but in everything by prayer and supplication with thanksgiving let your requests be made known unto God. And the peace of God, which surpasses all comprehension, shall guard your hearts and minds in Christ Jesus" (Philippians 4:6-7).

We're not to let anything throw us into a panic. "Be anxious for nothing" can be translated, "Don't worry about anything." Look at that again—it's a command, not a request. It's an important command that touches the grass root problems of life.

What happens when an emergency situation arises? The first reaction is to panic! Common sense tells us panic is not the correct reaction; nevertheless, we hit the "panic button." The Word tells us it's the wrong reaction, because panic is uncontrolled worry. Even though panic is a natural response, it's the wrong response.

"Okay, I've got it. Don't panic. But what do I do now?"

Paul continues by telling us to pray about the problem. ". . . but in everything by prayer and supplication with thanksgiving let your requests be made known to God." What are we doing when we pray about it? We are telling God our problem and inviting His concern and aid on our behalf. Our prayer is to be with thanksgiving—thanking God for two things: *First*, that we have the problem which forces us to recognize our dependence upon Him; *Second*, that we can come to Him with our problems.

Will that work? Of course it will. Paul goes on to tell us that when we commit the problem to God in prayer, our mental anguish will cease because His incomprehensible peace shall stand watch over our troubled hearts. Worry comes when there is mental anguish and is dispelled when God's peace floods our souls. Once we have committed our need to God. His peace stands military guard duty over our souls and is the antidote to worry.

During my first pastorate, I visited a woman just before she was wheeled into the operating room for major surgery. She knew her chances of surviving the surgery were about fifty-fifty. She was naturally concerned about her husband and two young children that would be left behind if she were to die. In those few moments, I shared with her this precious promise from the Word. When we prayed and committed her problem to the Lord, the nurses came to take her to surgery. When I visited her the next day, she shared this testimony: "Yesterday after we prayed and they wheeled me down the hallway to surgery, a wonderful peace came over me that I had never known before."

Summary

We all face pressures that are apt to produce worry. Unless we deal with worry, it will cause serious problems. But God makes it possible for us to move off the tollway of worry. We are commanded to:

1. Stop worrying and start trusting,
2. Stop straining and turn loose, and
3. Stop the panic and start praying.

Obey these three commands and watch worry dissolve.

CHAPTER 8

———◆———

"GOD . . . I'M DISAPPOINTED"

Growing up on my father's farm in Texas, I enjoyed looking at magazines depicting the beauties of California. I envisioned this state as one long sandy beach bathed by warm rays of sunshine every day of the year and dreamed of one day living there.

At last my opportunity came. After completing high school I entered the Navy; and after initial training, was elated to learn my first duty station was in California. Anticipation was high as I boarded my flight from Dallas one hot, sultry July afternoon bound for the land of sunshine and sandy beaches.

Six hours later the plane touched down in Oakland. It was fifty-three degrees and raining . . . in mid-July! I was crushed! As I rode along the Bay-shore Freeway in a bus to my duty station, I felt betrayed by the peddlers who promised sandy beaches and sunshine. There I was . . . chilled by the cold . . . and no beaches in sight! The cold summer rain dampened my enthusiasm for "sunny California" and taught me that things are not always what we envision.

Disappointment is one of the frustrating

problems each of us must face. Often I hear people say, "He disappointed me so much." Or have you ever said to someone, "I'm so disappointed in you."? Or even more pointed, "God ... I'm disappointed."

If we are to face life realistically, we will have to grapple with the problem of disappointment. It can't be ignored.

What happens inside when we say we are disappointed? The dictionary says it means "to be made unhappy by the failure of one's hopes or expectations." Disappointment then is the sinking feeling we get when our plans blow up in our faces.

From the beginning of history men have had their plans go awry (even great men of faith faced this). The Bible doesn't present these men of faith as cardboard characters with a perpetual smile. On the contrary, Scripture exposes the tender underside of their failures while painting the picture of their accomplishments. The pressing question is not *who* experiences disappointment, but *why?* What causes that sinking feeling when things don't pan out?

Disappointment generally falls into two distinct categories—circumstances and people.

When things are not as expected, we become disappointed. Abraham experienced this. One day while he was living in the rich alluvial basin around Ur of the Chaldees, God spoke to Abraham and directed him to leave his home for a new land He would show him. Instantly Abraham obeyed, taking his herds and immediate family on a thousand mile journey to this new land. I am sure as he made that long journey on foot, he developed expectation and high hopes about his new promised land.

But the Biblical record of his arrival tersely states: "Now there was a famine in the land. . . ." (Genesis 12:10).

No record is given to Abraham's feelings but it's reasonable to assume he was disappointed. As he sat in his tent he must have thought, "I left the beauty of Ur, all my relatives, walked a thousand miles, and what do I get—a land wasted by drought. This isn't what I expected."

Disappointment also comes when plans fall through. This frequently happens to parents. Often from the time their child is still an infant, many parents begin to plan the kind of career their child will enter, where he will go to school, and whom he will marry. Disappointment comes when the child announces he wants something different than what his parents planned.

When extensive plans for a vacation have to be cancelled, we are disappointed. But the most painful disappointment comes when people fail us.

Paul experienced this kind of disappointment. He arrived in Troas fully expecting to see Titus (2 Corinthians 2:12–14), but Titus was nowhere to be found. Titus' failure to keep the appointment caused Paul disappointment.

Disappointment comes when we trust a person to do something and he fails us. Moses experienced such a disappointment. God called him to deliver Israel from Egyptian bondage, but Moses begged off. "God, You know I'm not an eloquent speaker." Graciously God designated Aaron, his brother, as his mouthpiece. After deliverance was accomplished, Moses and Aaron were in the wilderness with the nation at Mt. Sinai. Moses then left the camp and went up in the mount to receive instructions from God concerning His laws. While there, God told Moses to get back down the mountain before He destroyed the people. Moses hurried back to the camp and found it in an uproar. The people had persuaded Aaron to build a golden calf and thus instituted idolatry. Imagine Moses' disappointment in Aaron and the people of Israel.

Disappointment is part of life, and it's important to know how to deal with it. Failure to cope with disappointment can be devastating.

The first consequence of unresolved disappointment is cynicism. A person in this state feels it's futile to rely on anybody; his confidence in people is at such a low ebb he'd rather not believe anything they say. "If I don't expect anything from them, they can't disappoint me."

Disappointment brings discouragement. Constant failure to realize our plans or expectations will cause us to lose confidence and hope, and inability to handle disappointment becomes a great tool for Satan. The following story by Walter Knight illustrates this.

It was advertised that the devil was going to put his tools up for sale. On the date of sale the tools were placed for public inspection, each being marked with its sale price. They were a treacherous lot of implements—Hatred, Envy, Jealousy, Deceit, Lying, Pride, and so on, comprised the outfit. Laid apart from the rest was a harmless-looking tool, well-worn, and priced very high.

"What is the name of this tool?" asked one of the purchasers pointing to it.

"That is Discouragement," tersely replied the devil.

"Why have you priced it so high?"

"Because it is more useful to me than the others. I can pry open and get inside a man's heart with that, when I cannot get near him with other tools. Once I get inside, I can make him do what I choose. It is badly worn because I use it on almost everyone, since few people know it belongs to me."

Disappointment will make us want to give up in despair. "What's the use? Nothing ever works out for me. Everything always goes wrong. I'm tired of getting my hopes up only to be let down." We will eventually want to crawl off in a corner and let the world go on by without attempting to be a part of it.

When disappointment comes, the tendency is to blame somebody else. The man behind bars says, "I got a raw deal." The man whose business fails says, "It's the banker's fault because he wouldn't loan me more money." The man who was passed over for promotion says, "It's the boss's fault because he didn't recognize my talents."

Blaming others for our disappointments is an admission that we have never learned to handle one of the basic problems of life. Failure to deal with disappointment leads to cynicism, discouragement, and despair.

The Bible sets forth several principles that when known and applied will keep disappointments from being a problem to you. (Not that disappointments won't come, but they won't get you down—you can take them in stride.)

Three basic principles are essential if we want to conquer disappointment. First: *Realize God is in control of ALL circumstances.* God is sovereign Ruler over the universe and cannot be overthrown. Because He is in control of all circumstances, the life of the believer cannot be a series of freak accidents. It is under the direction of the soverign God, and He makes no mistakes.

What is disappointment to one may well be what makes another happy. The rain at a picnic may make a boy unhappy because it ruined the picnic; on the other hand, it may make the father happy because he didn't want to go in the first place. Likewise, rain may make the boy happy because he doesn't have to mow the lawn; it may make the father unhappy because he wanted the lawn to be mowed. God *is* in control of circumstances that come our way—He makes no mistakes!

God has a definite plan for our lives . . . the very best possible. When we choose to adopt our own plans rather than His, we can look for disappointment. True happiness in the midst of disappointment comes when we know the failure of our plans is in God's control. We have our ideas, but God has a better idea.

A keen awareness that God is in control of circumstances leads to the realization that our disappointments are God's appointments. This will help us beat the "grin and bear it" approach to disappointments. God can use our frustrations for good, if we let Him.

Paul is an excellent example of this. His missionary journeys were cut short and his plans to preach in other regions thwarted by a long imprisonment. We might wonder, "If God was in control of circumstances, why did He permit the fiery Paul to be imprisoned? Think of the people he could have reached!"

This is one way to look at it, but God had a better idea. Paul's disappointment was God's appointment because in prison, Paul had time for God to reveal more of His word to him. During those days of disappointment, Paul penned the "Prison Epistles," thereby bequesting a rich legacy in the books of Ephesians, Philippians, and Colossians. These three epistles have been a blessing to multiplied millions, infinitely more than Paul could possibly reach had he been given another lifetime for missionary activity.

We often emphasize the statement from Hebrews that Jesus "endured the cross." But He did more than endure; He used the cross to bring about redemption for sinful man.

When God permits our well-laid plans to collapse, don't go around suffering like a good little scout. Consider it an opportunity to grow stronger and do something special for God. Out of our frustrations, God wants to make something good. God may have to let us fall flat on *our* plans before we will accept His plan. When disappointing circumstances force a change in our plans consider it a divine opportunity to do something special for God.

Second: *Recognize people for what they are —people*. This will save you great difficulty.

Jesus Christ never expected people to be any more than they are. He didn't suffer disappointment at the hands of men; He knew men's hearts.

He came to the Jewish nation and presented Himself with the credentials of Messiah. But the religious leaders—to show their appreciation to God—plotted His death on a cross. There He poured out His life for His followers . . . many of whom turned back from following Him because the way was too difficult.

The night before the cross, Peter, one of the inner three, bitterly spit out the words, "I don't know the Man." If ever there was a time when the darkness of disappointment would chill one's soul, it was then. But our Lord was never disappointed in men; He was a divine realist. He knew man's capacity, and never expected people to produce beyond their capability.

Following His first miracle, many people believed Jesus was the Messiah, but this didn't impress Jesus. He knew the fickleness of man's faithfulness:

> "Now when He was in Jerusalem at the Passover, during the feast, many believed in His name, beholding His signs which He was doing.
> But Jesus, on His part, was not entrusting Himself to them, for He knew all men,
> and because He did not need any one to bear witness concerning man for He himself knew what was in man" (John 2:23-25).

Jesus never put man on a pedestal. He knew the marks of a sin nature would always be present in man's actions. He refused to be carried away by the instant belief manifested over His first miracle. He had a realistic view of man which prevented disappointment.

Conversely, a realistic view of man will insulate you against disappointment when people let you down. It will keep you from looking for perfection in an imperfect specimen. Every person is capable of disappointing you if you let him. Don't expect people to be what they aren't—perfect! When you finally realize people are just people, it will make it easier to avoid condemning them for doing things that wreck your plans. With a correct view of man, you will not expect them to do more than they can do. (Incidentally, each one of us may bring disappointment to others. We're not certainly always the "wronged party"!)

A realistic view of man will keep us from becoming cynical. It will keep us from giving up on people. Let's face it—people are all we have to work with; let's not give up on them. But don't place your confidence in them either. Our confidence must rest in God, not the people God created.

When Paul came to Troas and didn't find Titus as prearranged, he was agitated. "I had no rest for my spirit . . . ." (2 Corinthians 2:13). But Paul didn't sit around and stew about being stood up; he forged ahead to Macedonia alone and found God led him in a continuous stream of triumph in Christ.

Third: *Remember our goal in life.* Our goal should be to "walk as He walked" (1 John 2:6). We need to pattern our life to conform to Jesus Christ. Hebrews 12:2 says it like this:

> "Fixing our eyes on Jesus the author and perfecter of faith, who for the joy set before Him endured the cross, despising the shame, and has sat down at the right hand of the throne of God."

Jesus Christ's goal was to seek and save those that were lost. A cross lay across the path toward that goal. But He was not turned aside from His goal by the suffering and shame of the cross; He endured the cross because He had His eyes firmly fixed on the goal—eternal redemption. Keeping His eyes on the goal of redemption did not lessen the agony involved, but it did enable Him to keep going until the task was accomplished!

Think about this for a moment. Keeping our eyes on our goal will keep us from being paralyzed by the frustration of disappointment. It will enable us to see beyond the circumstances and people to the prize. If we get our eyes on the disappointing situations, we will make little progress toward living our lives as Christ did.

The man who carries the football has one thing in mind—to get to the end zone. The linemen he faces are BIG and TOUGH. How many touchdowns would he score, if when he took the ball he thought, "Those guys really look mean."? Probably not many. The runner takes the ball, ducks his head, and drives right into the middle of the line on his way toward the end zone.

In the game of life, we face the big linemen disappointment. Don't become defeated; Jesus Christ has opened a hole for us to follow through the line. If we ever hope to keep from being defeated by disappointment, we'll have to keep our eye on the goal as we follow Jesus Christ.

We all face disappointment. Circumstances cause disappointment. People disappoint us. Were it not that God has made a way to escape, we would all be defeated.

Summary

When disappointment comes, we need to:

    1. Realize God is in control of ALL circumstances,

2. Recognize people for what they are—people, and
3. Remember our goal in life.

When the dark clouds of disappointment fill your sky, apply these simple principles and see how God will clear away the darkness of disappointment.

CHAPTER 9

———◆———

"GOD . . . I HAVE DOUBTS"

Frequently I hear people say, "When I get to heaven, I'm going to ask Paul what he meant when he said . . .", or, "I want to ask Peter what possessed him to deny the Lord the night of His trial"; or, "I want to ask the apostle John what it was like to be close to the Lord."

Many people desire to have an audience with some great man of the Bible in order to satisfy a personal curiosity. But I've never heard anyone say, "When I get to heaven, I want to talk with Thomas."

Why should anyone want to talk with Thomas? We know he is called "Doubting Thomas," and is the epitome of unbelief. What could we learn from him?

Nevertheless, we shouldn't write off Thomas because we probably have as much (or more!) in common with him than any other person in the Bible! He is the man whose faith faltered . . . who had honest questions and doubts concerning Jesus Christ. Because his problem is recorded, we can all learn from his experience.

Doubt is one of our daily tormenters. How often have you said, "I just don't believe it" . . .

"It just can't be" . . . "That's impossible" . . .
"That's a likely story."? Have you ever secretly said, "God . . . I have doubts?"

When we drop our masks of piety, we must
admit most of us are plagued with secret
doubts. Doubt is one of the destructive forces
constantly at work eroding our confidence in
ourselves and Christianity. Successful Christian living, however, dictates that we learn
how to cope with it.

Doubt has been called the unsettled feeling in
one's opinions or beliefs. It means one is in-
clined to unbelief (which is the antithesis of
belief or faith). It's the nagging inner feeling
that we will not be able to do what we've
planned, or what we have believed may not be
true after all.

Many things cause doubt. Calamities jar our
confidence in ourselves or the future. If a doctor
reports we have a terminal illness, it's a jar-
ring experience. We want to believe with all
our hearts that he's wrong, yet inwardly we
have no confidence in our future health.

When faced by an impossible situation,
doubts bubble to the surface, especially when
past failures shake our confidence in our abilities to undertake a new venture. A church
which has had nothing but struggles finds it
difficult to launch a new expansive program believing God can and will supply. The same is
true for an individual.

Failure to look beyond our natural abilities
and resources breeds doubt. Doubt inevitably

comes when we look at some of the situations we face and evaluate our resources for meeting them.

Many men (particularly those in their forties) lack confidence in themselves. As they join the era of the four B's, (baldness, bifocals, bridges, and bulges) they entertain fears of losing their virility and manhood and may seek reassurance by having a fling.

Television ads make us uneasy about our social acceptance. We are barraged by advice to use a certain mouthwash, toothpaste, or dandruff shampoo in order to make us socially acceptable. We succumb to their appeal and spend our money on confidence-producing products. But all the time we are with people, we wonder (in the words of one deodorant manufacturer) if "it's working."

Abraham and Sarah didn't think they were physically able to accomplish the staggering things God promised them. As Abraham approached one hundred and Sarah ninety, God reaffirmed the promise that they would have children (Genesis 18:10). Sarah's doubt concerning her ability to bear children at such an advanced age gave way to laughter. She really didn't believe God could do it.

The competitive atmosphere at work generates doubts. Many older men become unsure of their abilities to compete with the younger men. As years pass and their tasks become more complex, the question of abilities becomes more frequent. Doubts concerning ability to perform a task will hinder performance and halt promotions to higher levels of responsibility.

After years in a given career, some entertain second thoughts (doubts) as to whether or not it is the right career for them. They fear they will never amount to much in their given field of endeavor. As middle age approaches and promotions don't come as often, they begin to think about getting into another line of work.

John the Baptist had a moment like this. He spent his entire ministry preparing people for the coming of Jesus; he preached with great boldness condemning sin where he saw it (even in the palace of Herod); he pointed out Jesus Christ as the Messiah of Israel. But when Herod had him imprisoned, John entertained second thoughts concerning his life's work. Could it be that he had wasted his life? Two of his disciples were dispatched to Jesus secretly to ask if He was really the Messiah. ". . . Are You the Coming One, or shall we look for someone else?" (Matthew 11:3). To put it bluntly, John wanted to know, "Have I wasted my life for a cause that wasn't worth it?"

People have doubts about God. They ask, "Could God love someone like me?" . . . "Is the Bible really God's Word?" . . . "Can God help me with my problems?" Our personal doubts about God stem from our inability to believe God is interested in our problems.

Doubt gives us a nagging feeling that we can no longer rest in the power of God. We become a bundle of nerves with no confidence in anything. When confidence in God is gone, we can expect to live a tense, uneasy, and jumpy life, because we are left with only our own resources.

Doubts weaken our witness for Christ. People are desperate for something or someone they can believe. Having tried many unsuccessful cures for their ills, they are now ready to hear what God says and turn to the Christian to ask if it's real. But if we witness with "I hope" . . . "It may be" . . . "I think," they will not be interested. In witnessing for Christ, don't tell people your doubts; they have enough of their own!

Unresolved doubts condemn us to a life of mediocrity. The great men who were filled with doubts never became great because their potential for greatness was sabotaged by doubts. Their greatness simmered in the pot of doubts, leaving them in the category of those "who also ran."

"Thanks a lot!" you say. "Until you ripped the covers off, no one knew I had doubts; but now I've been exposed. My self-condemnation was bad enough, but having my doubts exposed really hurts."

It's not a sin for a Christian to have doubts; sin results when we persist in unbelief. Living with doubts shows we are failing to trust God. We don't have to live this way because God has made deliverance from doubts possible.

The best way to come to grips with doubts is to learn from one who has been there— "Doubting Thomas." An examination of

Thomas' experience (John 20:19–31) reveals some pertinent principles that, if followed, will enable us to escape the stronghold of doubt.

We learn four basic principles from Thomas. First: *Honestly admit our doubts.* Thomas *did!* After the resurrection, ten of the apostles were together in the upper room when Jesus made His first appearance to them. Thomas was absent. When he returned he found the ten in an uproar. "Thomas, guess what? We've seen the Lord; He was here in this room while you were gone!"

Thomas was unimpressed. "You fellows are putting me on. I don't believe you."

The ten persisted. "He's been resurrected and we've seen Him!"

Thomas probably reacted with, "Men, I'll be honest with you. Unless I see Him with my eyes and touch Him with my hands, I won't believe you."

He flatly rejected the testimony of the ten because he didn't believe it could happen. And the enthusiasm of the ten didn't seem to phase him. ". . . Unless I shall see in His hands the imprint of the nails, and put my finger into the place of the nails, and put my hand into His side, I will not believe" (John 20:25).

Give Thomas credit. He had the fortitude to stand up to the ten and say, "I don't believe you." He honestly admitted he didn't believe Jesus had risen.

What a striking lesson! If we ever hope to deal with doubt, we must reach the point where we are willing to honestly admit that we don't believe. Thomas wasn't willing to live out his life pretending to believe something he didn't. He couldn't smile and proclaim "He is risen" while not believing inside.

It is impossible to drown our doubts in the creeds of the church. Singing loudly (when our hearts don't believe what our mouths are saying) won't make them go away. Through the years the church has often communicated the idea that "nice people don't have doubts about God." As a result, people begin to suspect the church doesn't have answers to life's problems.

While in seminary, I worked on the freight docks. One of my co-workers was a sharp college boy named Jake—a self-professed skeptic and agnostic with a sarcastic attitude to those who claimed to be Christians. I worked with him for almost two years before Jake revealed why he believed the way he did. As a boy he attended Sunday School and church. But when he got to high school, questions about creation, science, and the Bible began to bother him. One day he went to see his pastor. "Why does the Bible say the earth was created in six days and scientists claim it's billions of years old? And what about the evolution of man? Who is right?"

The pastor's response was shattering: "We don't ask questions like that around here." And the pastor ushered Jake out of his study.

Jake got the message all right! Church is not a place where honest questions and doubts about God are discussed. He concluded the church did not have answers to the doubts that plague men; he left and never returned. A bright young mind was lost to the cause of Christ because his doubts were hushed when they should have been dealt with honestly. What a tragedy! Let the church come out of its bomb shelter and handle the honest doubts of people.

Until we are willing to honestly admit our doubts, we won't overcome them. When we are able to say, "I know I'm supposed to believe that, but I need proof," we're on the road to liberation from the tyranny of doubt.

During a rap session dealing with problems young people face, one high school senior put her finger on the pulse of the issue when she said, "From the time we were little, we believed certain things because our parents told us. But there comes a time in our life when we no longer believe something just because our parents tell us. We want to know why we should believe these things."

She admitted what everyone there knew. We all have doubts that must be satisfied by facts, not pious cliches from a church that is hiding its head in the sand.

Unless we are willing to honestly admit our doubts, we will continue to mouth the creeds of Christianity while inwardly saying, "I will not believe." We will be torn by what we know we should believe, but don't. Liberation begins when we honestly say, "God . . . I have doubts."

Second: We need to *rely on the fellowship and association of other believers*. Where was Thomas when the Lord appeared to the ten?

What he feared most happened—His Lord had been crucified; but instead of remaining with the other apostles, he sought refuge and consolation in isolation. In his absence, Christ came and Thomas missed his appointment with the Lord. The ten were enthusiastic about the resurrection because they were there and saw Him; but Thomas had set himself apart, and thus doubt quenched his joy.

We need the fellowship of other believers to strengthen our faith. Isolation from the assembly breeds and nourishes doubt. The longer we remain in isolation, the greater our doubts become. Experience in counseling has shown me that people who are infrequent attenders at church gatherings have far more doubts than those who fellowship with other believers. These occasional attenders (the "nod to God crowd") miss the encouragement to their faith that comes from being with other believers. It is no accident that we are exhorted "not forsaking our own assembling together, as is the habit of some" (Hebrews 10:25). Our faith is strengthened by the corporate, collective witness of other believers.

Third: We need to *remember the promises and power of God*. Apparently, Thomas forgot a promise Jesus often repeated. Jesus frequently spoke of the cross, but He always affirmed that He would rise again. In his personal grief, Thomas forgot the wonderful promise of the resurrection and was unable to believe the resurrection announcement.

Many doubts arise because we have either

forgotten or don't understand God's promises
concerning our problems. We are told in Scripture: "I can do all the things through Him
who strengthens me" (Philippians 4:13),
Don't be like Thomas; remember the promises
of God to you.

We also need to recount the power of God
that has already been demonstrated. Thomas
had been an eyewitness to many miracles: He
had seen water turned into wine; lepers
healed; blind eyes opened; the dead raised; but
when it came to the resurrection of Jesus
Christ, he said in effect, "God can do anything
but that." Every miracle should have prepared
him for that momentous occasion, but they
slipped his mind, and he refused to believe.

We face situations when prudence says we
best not raise our hopes too high. When a doctor says there is no hope we have a bad habit
of taking his word for it! We should not give
up hope so quickly. If we stop and recount the
times we've seen God turn impossible situations into happiness, the easier it will be for
us to say along with Abraham, "Is anything
too hard for God?" (Genesis 18:14). The only
justification we have for giving up is when we
rely on our own power rather than God's.
When doubts begin to rise, we need to remember the promises and power of God. The impossible situations are opportunities for the
Power of God to work.

Fourth: We need to *bring our doubts directly to the Lord*. Thomas wanted a personal
audience with the Lord Jesus. He heard the ten

declare the resurrection but was unwilling to accept their testimony without personal experience with Christ. For eight days Thomas wallowed in his doubts. Then Jesus came again: ". . . Peace be with you! Then He said to Thomas, Reach here your finger, and see My hand; and reach here your hand, and put it into My side; and be not unbelieving, but believing" (John 20:26, 27).

Our Lord in loving grace presented Himself to Thomas and invited his personal examination. We have no record of Thomas accepting the invitation. The next words record the worship of a now believing disciple. Thomas cried out, ". . . My Lord and my God" (John 20:28). The visible presence of christ was enough to dissolve Thomas' doubts, and he fell before His Lord in worship and adoration.

Jesus dealt tenderly with the doubts of Thomas. But He did not stop there; He added special benediction for believers in the centuries to follow. ". . . Because you have seen Me, have you believed? Blessed are they who did not see, and yet believed" (John 20:29). We are able to believe without a personal audience with Christ.

We can bring our doubts directly to God and have Him deal with them. When we cry out, "I don't know how God could love me," we can be reassured because of the visible reminder of the cross. It makes us fall in adoration and worship of Him who really loved us.

When we wonder, "Lord, what can you possibly do with me?" we know He did something with a man like Thomas and He can do something with us. When we bring our doubts directly to God, we will find He deals with our doubts in love and tenderness.

Summary

We have to admit we are at times plagued with paralyzing doubts. But at the same time, we know God has provided a way to deal with doubt. Through the experience of Thomas we know doubts can be dissolved if we will:

1. Honestly admit we have doubts,
2. Rely upon the fellowship of other believers,
3. Remember the promises and power of God, and
4. Bring our doubts directly to the Lord.

God delivered "Doubting Thomas" from his doubts. Why not come to Him and let Him deal with your doubts and restore you to effective service?

CHAPTER 10

———◆———

"GOD . . . I'M PROUD"

One afternoon Goethe and Beethoven chatted and strolled together in the Carlsbad Valley. As they walked, passersby saluted, pointed them out, and bowed with ostentatious deference.

"Isn't it maddening?" exclaimed Goethe. "I simply can't escape this homage."

"Don't be too much distressed by it," said Beethoven. "It is just possible that some of it may be for me."

If this story is true, Goethe, the great German poet, was suffering from a rather advanced case of pride! None dare question the poetic ability of Goethe; this is an established fact. But in the presence of an equally great man—Beethoven—to assume that the homage was to him alone was a mark of crass human pride. Beethoven did a masterful job of deflating Goethe's ego.

Pride afflicts many great men . . . and many not so great! It's easy for some to become wrapped up in their self-importance and think the world revolves around them. Other people, they believe, are around only to reflect their self-perpetuated glory. Someone has wisely said that the man who is wrapped up in his own self-importance makes a very small package! One can have world acclaim but not be truly great because of pride. The larger a man becomes in his own eyes, the smaller he becomes as a person, because self-importance works to obscure true greatness.

Is there anything that can be done to counter the problem of sickening pride? Yes, God has made it possible for us to deal with this problem. This should come as good news because pride is one of the ugliest of all human problems.

The dictionary says that pride is an over-high opinion of oneself. It is exaggerated self-esteem. Pride comes from the Greek word *phusioo* which means "to be puffed up, inflated" . . . the idea of a bellows used by the blacksmith to blow air on the coals and keep the fire going. Pride is being filled with hot air; being puffed up with the air of self-importance; having an inflated opinion of oneself. Josh Billings said that most people are like eggs—too full of themselves to hold anything else; or as someone said, "Pride is arrogant self-esteem."

Pride bears an unsavory reputation, but it also has a positive side. In the good sense, pride refers to dignity and self-respect. A person who doesn't possess the dignity of his own worth goes to the other extreme to false humility. Don't let the word pride rob you of your rightful dignity and self-respect.

But when a person becomes inflated with self-importance, he imitates Lucifer, the father of pride. Lucifer was beautiful when created by

God. He was given an honored place among the angels (Isaiah 14, Ezekiel 28). He was placed over all the angels receiving and transmitting glory to God.

One day he wanted to grab some of the glory for himself. He thought, "I will make myself like the Most High" (Isaiah 14:14b). He rebelled against God in an effort to boost his own career ahead of what God intended. Pride began in the heart of the fallen one, Lucifer, and all manifestations of pride since have been fueled by the fires of hell.

Pride causes us to become impressed with out own abilities. Given enough rope, pride will eventually make us think we are capable of operating independently of God; it makes us feel self-sufficient.

Pride falls into several different categories. We may succumb to the "pride of position" because of the job we hold. This is particularly true of many who have reached the place where they have a carpet on the floor and a title on the door!

"Pride of position" has a first cousin called "pride of organization." Churches are easy prey for this problem. Some put forth the confident assertion that "We are the *best* church in town." This is frequently used to foster *esprit de corps* among the members. However, these three words can be translated by one word—pride.

It's an error of the highest degree to suggest everyone should attend their church because it's the "best" in town. Such claims show a basic ignorance of a church personality. No one church is the right church for everyone in town because churches have different emphases in their ministry that serve the particular needs of those in attendance. Organizational pride originated in the pits of hell.

Another member of the family is the "pride of possessions." Unconsciously people often rate themselves as part of a certain social strata because of what they own—pride of living on the right side of the tracks, driving a prestige automobile, or belonging to the country club. People struggle to own things that outwardly inflate their egos. The more material possessions we own, the more we must be on guard against pride of possessions.

A fourth member of the family is called "pride of intellect." The modern world has gone berserk over knowledge and learning. A Bachelor's Degree is no longer sufficient to command favored position in the job market. Now, one must have an M.A. or Ph.D. In our age of dialogue, many Christians have become overly impressed with their degrees. Christians should strive to be as well educated as possible, but at the same time be on guard against the pride of intellect.

The last child in the family is called "pride of accomplishment," or as the apostle John calls it, "the pride of life" (1 John 2:16). It's an ever present danger to view success as a result of our own personal efforts rather than the blessing of God. It is easy to be humble when faced with failure, but difficult to do so in the hour of triumph and success; it's easy to depend on God when we are at the bottom, and easier still to depend on ourselves when we are at the top. When success arrives, the temptation is to tell God to go help someone else because we are now able to go it alone.

A farmer knows only certain kinds of plants grow in a certain type of soil at a certain altitude and a certain season of the year. Unfortunately, pride is hearty and thrives in any climate . . . any time of the year . . . at any altitude . . . in any area of the world. Look closely and you'll find pride of position, possessions, intellect, or accomplishment growing all around you.

When you go to the doctor with a problem, one of the first things he wants to know is your symptoms. Once he knows them, he is on the track of finding the cause of your illness.

Pride, like a medical malady, has symptoms that are easily detected. One case study in pride is the church at Corinth; a cursory glance reveals several tell-tale signs of pride.

One symptom of pride is the development of cliques. Paul struck right in the middle of this clique-oriented church when he declared, "For you are still fleshly. For since there is jealousy and strife among you, are you not fleshly, and are you not walking like mere men? For when one says, 'I am of Paul,' and another, 'I am of Apollos . . .'" (1 Corinthians 3:3-4) ; ". . . that in us you might learn not to exceed what is written, in order that no one of you might become arrogant in behalf of one against the other (1 Corinthians 4:6).

Pride results when we follow men rather than a ministry. The Corinthians were guilty of pride in their man which caused contention within the church. Someone said, "You can't raise turkeys and peacocks in the same area because both are strutters." When we begin to follow individual men, cliques develop within the church.

The tendency to gloss over sin is another symptom of pride. Gross immorality was prevalent in the church at Corinth; so gross it made the Gentiles blush. Instead of being grieved and taking action to root out the immorality, Paul said the Corinthians had ". . . become arrogant, and have not mourned instead, in order that the one who had done this deed might be removed from your midst" (1 Corinthians 5:2). A flagrant case of immorality was permitted to exist in the church because the believers were too arrogant to deal with this sin. Pride obscures our ability to see things as they really are.

A third symptom of pride is a lack of concern for others. The Corinthians used their liberty in Christ with such an uncaring attitude that young believers were damaged.

> "But take care lest this liberty of yours somehow become a stumbling block to the weak.
> For if someone sees you who have knowledge dining in an idol's temple, will not his

conscience, if he is weak, be strengthened to eat things sacrificed to idols?

For through your knowledge he who is weak is ruined, the brother for whose sake Christ died" (1 Corinthians 8:9-11).

A person filled with self-importance will demand his own way or rights, regardless of the effect on others. Pride makes it easy to rationalize one's own importance and make everyone else subservient to his wishes.

Pride is deadly! It doesn't come into our lives with the force of a freight train. It doesn't come up and say, "My name is pride. How about me sharing your life?" It slips in subtly and continues to inflate the ego until it has a stranglehold. By the time its sinister presence is realized, pride may have delivered the *coup de grace* to your testimony and spiritual life.

The Word of God sets forth three basic principles which, if followed, will deflate our balloon of pride.

First: *Be alert to the dangers of pride.* When allowed to exist, Satan will use it to defeat us. "Pride goes before destruction, and a haughty spirit before stumbling" (Proverbs 16:18).

Paul made it clear that a young convert should not be chosen for roles of leadership; maturity is a prerequisite for leadership. "And not a new convert, lest he become conceited and fall into the condemnation incurred by the devil" (1 Timothy 3:6). A young believer is more apt to become impressed with his own self-importance if elevated to a position of leadership. When this happens, it is a rerun of Satan's rebellion against God.

Failures of others are recorded in the Bible as divine object lessons. Paul detailed some of the failings of the children of Israel (1 Corinthians 10) as object lessons on "how not to live."

When confronted by the bitter failures of someone else, we face a danger of letting pride put words in our mouth such as, "Isn't that awful . . . I would never have thought he would do that . . . I would never do that!" Paul drives home an important point when he says, "Therefore let him who thinks he stands take heed lest he fall" (1 Corinthians 10:12). We walk along a narrow ledge and are just as apt to fall into the same sins as those we quickly condemn. The minute you think you are beyond the devil's reach, the fall is just around the corner because pride makes you vulnerable.

Second: *Be honest with yourself and God.* Take a good look at yourself in light of God's Word, and you'll discover God has a different opinion of your capacities than you do. If you want an honest evaluation of what you are really like, read the Word of God (not your autobiography). The Bible doesn't give a touched up version of man; like a mirror, it tells it like it really is. Any man who sees himself as someone to be admired makes it evident he has not given much thought of God's evaluation of himself.

Paul gives an unvarnished treatment of the

basic nature of all men in his epistle to the Romans. Listen to his description of us in chapter three.

> "THERE IS NONE RIGHTEOUS, NOT EVEN ONE.
> THERE IS NONE WHO UNDERSTANDS,
> THERE IS NONE WHO SEEKS FOR GOD;
> ALL HAVE TURNED ASIDE, TOGETHER THEY HAVE BECOME USELESS;
> THERE IS NONE WHO DOES GOOD,
> THERE IS NOT EVEN ONE.
> THEIR THROAT IS AN OPEN GRAVE,
> WITH THEIR TONGUES THEY KEEP DECEIVING,
> THE POISON OF ASPS IS UNDER THEIR LIPS;
> WHOSE MOUTH IS FULL OF CURSING AND BITTERNESS;
> THEIR FEET ARE SWIFT TO SHED BLOOD,
> DESTRUCTION AND MISERY ARE IN THEIR PATHS,
> AND THE PATH OF PEACE HAVE THEY NOT KNOWN. THERE IS NO FEAR OF GOD BEFORE THEIR EYES" (Romans 3:10-18).

Don't try to escape by saying Paul is describing the pagans in his day. Go back and read the statement of universality like "none" and "all." Yes, God includes all of us in His description of what man is really like.

Incidentally, the Bible's description of man is a good argument for the divine inspiration of Scripture. No man in his right mind would write a book containing such a universal condemnation of himself. Man wouldn't, but God did!

We can't bypass the effects of our "badness" by being super good. Some might try to circumvent the awfulness of their nature by doing loads of good deeds. Isaiah set God's stamp of disapproval on all our self-help projects: "For all of us have become like one who is unclean, and all our righteous deeds are like a filthy garment. . . ." (Isaiah 64:6).

Do you take rags used to wipe up grease and lay them up in the closet with your best linens? The filthy rags of our righteousness will never, and can never, be placed in God's "linen closet" of righteousness.

A word of caution. While being realistic about who we are, we are to evaluate ourselves honestly. Even though we are not what we might think, we are somebody. He says, "For through the grace given to me I say to every man among you not to think more highly of himself than he ought to think; but to think so as to have sound judgment, as God has allotted to each a measure of faith" (Romans 12:3).

This reminds us that we are somebody, not just a speck of dust in the totality of a vast universe.

Realizing we are somebody, we are to take an honest look at who we are in the sight of God. While we are not to overthink (*huperphroneo*), we are not to underthink either. We are to exercise sound judgment concerning ourselves. Sound judgment (*sophroneo*) means "to be in one's right mind." One man suggested Paul treats pride as a species of insanity. Failure to agree with the evaluation of yourself in the Word of God is pride.

The story is told of a young girl who confessed to the Catholic priest she had incurred the sin of vanity.

"What makes you think that?" he asked.

"Because every morning when I look into the mirror," she replied, "I think how beautiful I am."

"Never fear," said the priest, "that isn't a sin—that's just a mistake."

Third: *Be thankful to God for what you are.* If you have attained anything, give the glory to God because it came from Him in the first place.

Thank God for your position as a gift from Him. In the famous passage on the vine and branches, Jesus declared, ". . . for apart from Me you can do nothing" (John 15:5).

Promotions do not come from the employer, but from God. They are not based upon one's super ability, but upon His grace. When promoted, it is right and proper to acknowledge the role of the employer; but he is only fulfilling the decree of God.

Position in life is a grace gift from God. If you have been blessed with a high salaried job with prestige, great! Give God the credit for placing you where you are. If your job is one of lesser means, praise God who has placed you in the best possible position for you.

Our possessions likewise come from God. James makes this clear: "Every good thing bestowed and every perfect gift is from above, coming down from the Father of light, with whom there is no variation, or shifting shadow" (James 1:17). Possessions do not result from our native abilities and shrewd planning, but from God's grace. Now it doesn't mean we are not to plan properly. It means we are receivers of God's gifts, not the originators. Since God gave them, we have no basis for an inflated opinion of ourselves based on our possessions.

Wisdom is also God's gift (not our brainpower): "But if any of you lacks wisdom, let him ask of God, who gives to all men generously and without reproach, and it will be given to him" (James 1:5). God is the dispenser of wisdom to His creatures: "For who regards you as superior? And what do you have that you did not receive? But if you did receive it, why do you boast as if you had not received it?" (1 Corinthians 4:7). The differences between men is a result of the creative activity of God.

Face the facts. What we are and have are visible results of God's grace. Since we received these blessings from God, what right do we have to be puffed up with pride? None! Take some practical advice from the words of Paul: "But may it never be that I should boast, except in the cross of our Lord Jesus Christ, though which the world has been crucified to me, and I to the world" (Galatians 6:14).

Spend time giving glory to God for His act of love at Calvary, and you will not have time to puff up your own ego. Rather, you will be drawn up short in worship of the Lord God. Self-glory is strangely out of place when you are giving glory to Christ—the only one who deserves any glory.

Summary

If we aren't careful pride might sneak into our lives, and before we know it, we'll be puffed up with a bad case of self-importance. If this should happen to you, you can deflate that ego if you will:

1. Be alert to the dangers of pride,
2. Be honest with yourself and God and
3. Be thankful to God for what you are in His sight.

If you will follow these three steps, you will find it easy to deal with the nasty problem of pride.

CHAPTER 11

───────◆───────

"GOD . . . I'M AFRAID"

As a country boy in Texas, my four brothers and I had a regular round of chores. One of my chores during the winter months was to bring in a bucket of corn cobs to be used as kindling to start the fire in the fireplace.

Occasionally I would get involved in something and forget. But it never failed, my father would check just before bedtime to see if the corn cobs were there by the fireplace. If I had forgotten, he would send me out to the barn alone to get them.

The barn was about a hundred yards from the house (about the longest hundred yards I can ever remember!), with no street lights, or handy flashlight; and it was dark! Every time I had to go out in that blackness I was petrified! I just knew some wild animal would jump out of the hayloft and eat me up before I could fill the bucket!

No one ran a hundred yards, filled a bucket full of corn cobs, and returned faster than I did! Each time I broke my previous record—fear spurred me on, and it usually took an hour for my heart to settle back to normal rhythm.

I thought I would get rid of fear as I grew older. But because fear is one of the base emotions of the human heart, we never seem to be completely free of it.

The dictionary gives three different shades of meaning to fear: (1) Fear is a feeling of anxiety and agitation caused by the presence or nearness of danger. Practially speaking, it's the feeling you get in the pit of your stomach when you're called in to see the boss after doing something wrong! (2) Fear is a feeling of uneasiness. For example, when your teenager isn't in by curfew, you're afraid something has happened to him. (3) Fear is also a feeling of a respectful awe or dread . . . as when you encounter a snake.

In his book, *The Psychology of Jesus and Mental Health,* Raymond Cramer said, ". . . fear is an emotional response which is consciously recognized, stimulated usually by some real threat." Fear is the tense feeling which grips you when you are faced with the tough problems of life. Have you ever felt your emotions were like taut guitar strings? Fear stretches your emotions and leaves you feeling wound up.

In the New Testament, three different words are translated fear; (1) *Deilia* which is always used in a negative sense. It is used of those who denied the faith under duress. It is the anxiety that comes from pressures. (2) *Phobos* (from which we get the English word "phobia") is more neutral. Sometimes it's good for a person to have phobias. Fear in the presence of danger is a good type of phobia. (3) *Eulabeia* indicates reverence toward God. It is always used in a good sense; as in Hebrews 12:28: "Therefore, since we receive a kingdom which cannot be shaken, let us show gratitude, by which we may offer to God an acceptable service with reverence and awe."

In this chapter I want to focus on the negative aspect (*deilia*) of fear.

People are afraid of many things—the dark, high places, the unknown, other people, failure, bad breath, of not being accepted by God, the day of judgment. Our minds can't be at rest when fear is pumping adrenalin into our system with the signal to "fight" or flee."

In recent years, doctors have found that some fears are caused by physiological problems. When the human system is out of balance, fears may result. A person who suffers from constant fears should first see his doctor for a thorough checkup.

But most fears can be traced back to a spiritual problem because the ultimate cause of fear is sin. The first record of fear in the human race is in Genesis 3. Adam and Eve were placed in God's beautiful garden where He had fellowship with them and came to see them every day. It was a beautiful relationship. Then one day as God came looking for Adam and Eve, they were nowhere to be found.

God called out to Adam, "Where are you?"

Adam replied from the bushes where he and Eve were hiding, " . . . I heard the sound of

Thee in the garden, and I was afraid . . . so I hid myself" (Genesis 3:9–10).

Afraid? Why should Adam be afraid of God, his creator and friend? He had disobeyed God, and now fear gripped his soul. The immediate consequence of sin is fear of God.

Paul tells us that God established governments and we are to be subject to them. As long as we are doing what is right, we have no reason to be afraid of the government. But the rebellious citizen who has violated a command of God should be afraid of the authorities; they are God's ministers to execute wrath upon the evil doer (Romans 13:4). "If you want to dance," says an old saying, "you will have to pay the fiddler." Fear is one of the consequences of rebellion against God and government.

Fear does not originate with God, "For God has not given us the spirit of timidity, but of power and love and discipline" (2 Timothy 1:7). Since fear doesn't come from God, it must come from Satan, and it's one of his best tools to make you ineffective for God.

Sin causes fear! (But that doesn't mean every fear is a sin.) We don't want to face God when we have sinned against Him. We don't want to face our parents when we have disobeyed them. We don't want to face the boss when we have failed to carry out our assigned responsibilities. Why are we afraid? Because we haven't done what we know we should. We have disobeyed—and the resulting consequence is fear.

Chronic fear wreaks havoc in our lives; ". . . fear involves punishment. . . ." (1 John 4:18). When fear is present, we suffer penalties; fear produces physical, emotional, and spiritual problems.

In the physical realm, fear can limit the normal life span. People live under the constant threat of heart failure, and one of its chief culprits is hypertension. Research concerning this silent killer reveals that tensions and fears are contributing causes. Unresolved fear will add to our tension and perhaps be a factor in cutting short our three-score and ten. It can also limit many enjoyable activities. How many people do you know who are afraid to fly in an airplane?

Fear will cause a person to withdraw from daily activities. Some people have phobias that cause them to hide in their houses and not come out. Their life activities are circumscribed by fears.

Fear also creates emotional problems and impairs a person's ability to reason logically. What happens when we panic? We can't think straight; we're too busy trying to swallow our hearts to think logically.

Fear can produce a persecution complex. I know some people who think everyone is out to get them. Every time they hear a siren they're sure the police are coming for one of the family, or an ambulance is carrying a family member to the hospital. That kind of fear will put you through an emotional wringer.

Fear causes spiritual problems and paralyzes faith. As long as fear is allowed to persist, our effectiveness for God is limited. Faith will banish fear, or else fear will banish faith. Some become so afraid that not only can they not trust God for something big, they can't even trust Him for their daily bread. Fear causes many spiritual paralytics.

Fear condemns you to a life of immeasurable misery, and few things are as unbecoming and pathetic as a miserable child of God. (Even the misery of a non-Christian cannot compare to that of the child of God who is heir of the universe, power, love, and wisdom of God!)

We know we're not supposed to be afraid, but our efforts to "kick the habit" are fruitless. We cry out, "Why can't I quit being afraid? I know I'm to 'fear not,' but I don't know how to obey God's command. How can I stop?"

God's solution for fear deals with unnecessary fears. We should have a respect or dread of danger. To walk off a ten-story building is not fearlessness; it's foolishness. We are supposed to maintain a reverential awe (or fear) of God. God's solution for fear deals with the inner tension that comes to tear us apart emotionally, physically, and spiritually. Three things are essential in coping with fear.

First: *Realize fear is not part of God's program for us*. We are told emphatically to "fear not." Likewise, we are commanded to be "bold" —boldness is the opposite of fear.

Since fear is not part of God's plan, we are to do something about it. We can't escape it by taking a daily dose of tranquilizers, nor by a weekly visit to the psychotherapist. We can't defeat our fears by taking a rest at the Sheraton where "busy executives unwind." Deliverance from fears begins with a correct mental attitude.

Second: *Recognize we do not face our problems alone.* It makes no difference how severe our problems become, we are not alone. God does not jump out of the boat and leave us to "paddle our own canoe" when the going gets rough. God is with us when danger approaches. God is with us even when our personal safety is threatened. The survival instinct is a powerful drive and most people will do anything to stay alive. Even though we have the prospect of leaving this life and being with Christ which is far better, most of us are in no hurry to do so.

One pastor preaching on going to heaven issued this unique invitation, "All those who want to go to heaven, stand up."

Everyone in the church stood up except a little man on the front pew.

"Sir, don't you want to go to heaven?" asked the preacher.

"Yes," the man replied.

"Then why didn't you stand up with the rest of the people?"

"Oh, I thought you were making up a load to go tonight!"

Most people want to go to heaven, but are in no hurry to catch the flight!

Our Lord gave some pertinent advice to His disciples when they learned they would face problems and persecutions. ". . . do not fear those who kill the body. . . ." (Matthew 10:28). Why shouldn't we be afraid of those who are able to kill us? We are going to die anyway, so why fear those who have the power to bring about death?

We are not to fear those who have the axe or gun to rob us of our physical house. Rather Jesus instructs us to fear the one who has the power to kill the soul. The body is temporal; the soul eternal. The only justifiable fear is divine fear, because God deals in eternal matters. We need not fear men who can hurt the body because God is the keeper of the soul.

Many people are anxious and concerned about their personal worth. Jesus made it clear the real worth is measured by God, not those around us. It is nice when our peers confirm our value, but it is nothing to get uptight about it they don't.

Quit worrying about what you're worth to those around you; their evaluation isn't what counts. God is the one who places the value on your personal worth.

Jesus continued His comforting words to the disciples:

> "Are not two sparrows sold for a cent? And yet not one of them will fall to the ground apart from your Father.
> But the very hairs of your head are all numbered. Therefore do not fear; you are of more value than many sparrows." (Matthew 10:29–31).

Even insignificant little sparrows are of value to God; He takes note when one of them falls. But we are of more value than many sparrows. It doesn't matter what value other men place on our lives. We are worth something to God. He is with us always to take care of His investment.

God is with us even though we may only have a few of this world's possessions. People have the tendency to be fearful in the presence of those who have great material fortunes. We fret and stew about what we have or don't have, as though it were important to God.

"Let your way of life be free from the love of money, being content with what you have; for He Himself has said, 'I WILL NEVER DESERT YOU, NOR WILL I EVER FORSAKE YOU' (Hebrews 13:5). We are not to be afraid; regardless of what we have, be content. This is a radical departure from contemporary philosophy which says "get more and more and more."

The writer goes on to say, "So that we confidently say, 'THE LORD IS MY HELPER, I WILL NOT BE AFRAID. WHAT SHALL MAN DO TO ME?'" (Hebrews 13:6). Once we recognize God is involved in our lives, our point of reference will change from the temporary to the eternal. God's omnipotent presence with us when we face problems will remove the poison darts of fear.

Finally: *We need to rest in the peace Christ gives*. Peace means a "mind at ease." Jesus

Christ promised us His relaxed mental attitude toward life's harried moments.

"It's hard to comprehend Christ's example of peace in the face of problems and danger. He knew better than anyone the kind of agony and suffering He would have to endure on the cross. But with assurance from God and a relaxed mental attitude, He endured the taunts and abuses heaped upon Him because He knew He was carrying out God's will. He faced agony with His mind at ease and thus left a perfect example of a life lived without fear.

The night before His death on the cross, Jesus gathered the disciples together in the upper room for farewell instructions. In the midst of the discourse, Jesus said, "Peace I leave with you; My peace I give unto you; not as the world gives, do I give to you" (John 14:27).

After giving the example of peace. He then made it possible for His followers to know the same relaxed attitude.

After the promise of peace, He urged them to rest on His peace: "Let not your heart be troubled, nor let it be fearful" (John 14:27). When we can relax in His peace, we will not be ripped to emotional shreds by the shears of daily tensions and problems. When we allow fear to invade and sear our lives, we admit we're not utilizing the relaxed mental attitude Jesus promised us.

He doesn't guarantee to immunize or keep us

from danger and problems; but He does guarantee peace in the midst of danger. Most of us frantically pursue protection from the problems rather than seek God's peace through them. We desperately cry out to God for deliverance but seldom pray for a relaxed mental attitude. Seeking deliverance rather than peace may cause us to miss the lesson God wants to teach us. The next time the bottom falls out, instead of asking God to put the bottom back in, ask Him to grant you the ability to relax and enjoy His peace.

We all face pressures that produce anxiety, uneasiness, and fear. We can't stop the pressures, but we can learn to deal with them.

Summary

If we want to live above the anxiety producing circumstances, we will have to:

1. Realize fear is not part of God's plan for our lives,
2. Recognize we do not face our problems alone—God is with us, and
3. Rest in the peace of Christ.

When fear seeks to paralyze your life, let God bring you out of its darkness into the light of His peace.

CHAPTER 12

———◆———

"GOD . . . I DON'T WANT TO DIE"

The wealthy householder sent his servant into the markets of Baghdad to buy food for a banquet. When the servant came to the market place he saw Death. Terrified, he fled and returned to his master and said, "Master, I just saw Death in the market place. Let me borrow your horse and flee into Syria where I will hide in a cave."

Later the same day the master went to the market place and he too saw Death. He approached Death and said, "Death, why did you frighten my servant so today?" "Oh," said Death, "I didn't mean to frighten him. In fact I was surprised to see him here, for I have an appointment with him tonight in a cave in Syria."

The servant in this story is typical of the many people who do everything within their power to flee the presence of death. Few people are willing to understand that death is part of life.

Death is not usually the topic of conversation during a New Year's Eve Ball or any other party. People who are having fun are not interested in discussing morbid subjects.

127

Have you noticed the tone of a conversation changes when death is mentioned? People become nervous and edgy; they hope by ignoring death it will go away. Even in the last moments of life, there is the struggle to avoid death and a cry to God for the continuation of life.

Whether we are willing to discuss or even think about it, death is a subject we will ultimately have to face, because all have an appointment with death.

Most people fear death, and even Christians frequently express uneasiness at the thought of dying. Why? Because death is unknown; and anytime we face something unknown or strange, we experience tension or foreboding.

After the resurrection, Jesus talked about life, not death. He didn't spend the forty days telling the disciples what they could expect the moment life ceased and they entered the other side. He spent time talking about what they were to do with their lives.

Another reason we fear death is the dread of facing God. We know we will have to stand before God to answer for our lives and are painfully aware we have not lived as we should nor done all we could. The thought of seeing our lives put on God's instant replay screen is chilling!

The *San Francisco Chronicle* reported a call girl as saying, "I am in great fear of death. I could not face God unless I had a chance to reform before my life was up." She expressed the innate fear of most people.

Death is something people desperately seek to avoid or delay regardless of cost. Millions are being poured into research in an effort to deter or defeat the grim reaper. People want new hearts, new kidneys and other "spare parts" that will enable them to prolong life. If this mad pursuit is continued, hospitals will have a "parts" department just like the auto shop! Medical science may prolong life, but in the end, death always wins.

People invest fortunes in an effort to stay death's hand for a short while longer. Just before Thomas Hobbs, an English skeptic, died, he said, "If I had the whole world, I would give it to live one day . . . ."

People frantically search for that eternal fountain of youth. Women try to find it in an assortment of creams and oils. But alas, time marches on and their faces and figures show the weight of years. Men, too, fight off the approaching of the forties. They dye their hair and get a young girlfriend, but their aching muscles tell them that old age cannot be delayed—time marches on! Each generation ignores the facts while seeking a way to remain forever young.

Since no one is anxious to die, how do we account for the increasing number of suicides? The man who commits suicide doesn't want to die; he wants an escape from misery. Suicide is not a desire for death; it's a frantic rebellion against society and the aging of life. The suicide victim would avoid it if he could find an alternative to his miserable life.

In spite of the fear of death, it is part of life because life is temporary. The prophet Isaiah described life as a tender succulent plant that is exposed to the scorching sun:

> ". . . All flesh is grass, and all its loveliness is like the flower of the field.
> The grass withers, the flower fades, When the breath of the Lord blows upon it; Surely the people are grass.
> The grass withers, the flower fades, But the word of our God stands forever" (Isaiah 40:6–8).

Crops in the early morning summer dew look fresh and crisp, but by mid-afternoon the burning heat causes the same plants to wilt and droop. Life is like that; we begin fresh, but with the weight of years, we wilt and fade away.

James uses a different figure to describe the transient nature of life. ". . . You are just a vapor that appears for a little while and then vanishes away" (James 4:14). Think about it—your life is no more than the early morning mist that is burned away by the sun.

Death is a reminder of man's rebellion against God. Man was created to live forever, but after his rebellion, he lost that right. He was evicted from the Garden which prevented him from partaking of the tree of life. Eating the forbidden fruit brought man the curse of death. Never has so much been lost by so little. Adam and Eve lost the right to physical life, and the forces of death began to tug at their bodies.

But more than physical life was lost in Eden. Adam and Eve experienced spiritual death long before their physical demise. They experienced spiritual death when they were driven from God's presence in Eden. Actually physical death was a blessing. It would be an unimaginable torment to live forever in bodies cursed by sin—subject to disease and infirmities.

Each time we read the obituary notices or see the funeral coach pass, we see a grim reminder that the penalty of sin is being exacted.

Each of us has a divine appointment with death that can't be ignored. Since death is certain, do we need to be afraid? No! God has made it possible for us to face death unafraid.

The only person who has any reason to fear death is the one who has never by faith trusted Christ as his personal Saviour. But once you have, you no longer need to fear death.

An examination of God's Word reveals several provisions that make it possible for the Christian to face death unafraid. These provisions are designed to give comfort and confidence in the face of death.

First: We need to *view death as the steppingstone to eternity*. ". . . it is appointed for men to die once, and after this comes judgment" (Hebrews 9:27). Regardless of the length of life, our days are numbered. The Psalmist says, "As for the days of our life, they contain sev-

enty years, Or if due to strength, eighty years.
. . ." (Psalms 90:10). Three thousand years
ago the age span of man was set at seventy
years. Today with all our medical research,
the current life span for a man is 67.7 years
while a woman's is seventy-four. These av-
erage out to be just over seventy. Medical
science hasn't been able to do much to delay
our appointment with the grim reaper.

Death introduces us to the first phase of
eternity—judgement! Life is a series of opportunities in preparation for the day of judgement. The first thing you will do in eternity
will be to give an accounting of the steward-
ship of your life. Preparation for that event
must be made during life.

Eternity begins when life ends. Death is the
doorway to eternity through which we must
pass to experience eternal life. It has been said
that life begins at forty, but this isn't true. We
have to die before life really begins!

Second: We need to *see that death repre-
sents a promotion*. Most people think of death
as the destruction of all we hope for. How can
we say that death is a promotion? Death ushers
us into the presence of Christ.

> "Therefore, being always of good courage,
> and knowing that while we are at home in the
> body we are absent from the Lord—
> For we walk by faith, not by sight—
> we are of good courage, I say, and prefer
> rather to be absent from the body and to be at
> home with the Lord" (2 Corinthians 5:6-8).

As long as we walk around in the house called our body, we are earth-bound, separated from Christ. But the moment we die, our house (body) drops away and we are ushered into the presence of the Lord. This tremendous truth is the basis of Paul's good courage. He faced the prospect of death every day. Without a divine perspective, he could have been glum and depressed, but he wasn't. He saw death as the usher who would bring him to the presence of Christ. Be of good cheer, death takes us to be with the Lord!

Paul goes on to say that dying is better than living. He wasn't a morbid, withdrawn skeptic who was miserable in life. On the contrary, he was filled with zest and enthusiasm for life. Life was great, but he anticipated something greater—death. Listen: "For to me, to live is Christ, and to die is gain" (Philippians 1:21). Even though he was stoned, imprisoned, and beaten for preaching the gospel, he was consumed with the passion of living for Christ. But as he thought about what lay beyond death, he said that is gain.

The knowledge that dying is better than living creates a tension in life. He said, ". . . I am hard pressed from both directions, having the desire to depart and be with Christ, for that is very much better; yet to remain on in the flesh is more necessary for your sake" (Philippians 1:23–24). Paul never hinted that death represented a bleak fearful prospect. He anticipated the promotion of death!

Be careful here. Just because death promotes us to the presence of Christ, we are not to rush out into the freeway and flirt with death. Life has a purpose. The only reason we are here on the earth now instead of in heaven with Christ is that we have a task to complete before going home.

Life is great! Live it to the full, but don't let your zest for life obscure your vision of the promotion that comes the moment you leave this life on earth.

Third: *Remember death has been conquered by life.* The dictionary is incorrect when it defines death as a permanent ending of life. The Bible makes it clear that death is not a permament ending of life; it is a transfer to another sphere of life.

Jesus Christ is life and His life conquers death. "In Him was life; and the life was the light of men" (John 1:4). "I am the resurrection and the life. . . ." (John 11:25). "I am the way, and the truth, and the life. . . ." (John 14:6).

Once we realize that Jesus Christ abolished death, it removes the sting and power of death. Paul tells us, "The sting of death is sin, and the power of sin is the law; but thanks be to God, who gives us the victory through our Lord Jesus Christ" (1 Corinthians 15:-56–57).

Tombstones in the cemetery are visible reminders of the power of sin to kill the body. But when we lay loved ones in the ground, we can be comforted in the knowledge that Jesus

Christ passed through physical death and came back victorious, defeating death. Death is no longer the sovereign king over man.

Summary

Death has everyone in its appointment book. We have no idea when our number will come up, but this is no reason for pessimism, gloom, or fear. God has made it possible for us to face death unafraid. You can be free from fear of death if you:

2. View death as the steppingstone to eternity,
2. View death as a promotion,
3. Remember that death has been conquered by life.

Knowing this and Jesus Christ allows us to face life and death unafraid!

APPENDIX

A SUMMARY OF HOW TO DEAL WITH YOUR PROBLEMS.

Depression

1. Get away from the problem for a rest.
2. Get your frustrations off your chest—tell God about it.
3. Get a fresh awareness of the personal presence of God.
4. Get back to work.

Temptation

1. Recognize it for what it is—an attempt to get you to rebel against God.
2. Realize God has given you the power to resist temptation.
3. Use the Word of God as your defense each time Satan comes and suggests a new rebellion.

Guilt

1. Accept that complete forgiveness is possible.

136

   2. Accept that God forgets when He forgives.

   3. Accept yourself as God does.

Boredom

1. Recognize boredom is not part of God's plan for your life.
2. Realize what you are doing is God's will for you.
3. Personalize your work; do it as a favor for Christ.

Loneliness

1. Realize you are never alone.
2. Realize there are other people in the same boat.
3. Get involved in God's program.

Bitterness

1. Recognize bitterness for what it is—sin.
2. Try to keep from hurting others (display human kindness).
3. Practice human forgiveness according to the divine standard.

Worry

1. Stop worrying and start trusting.
2. Stop straining and turn loose.
3. Stop the panic and start praying.

Disappointment

1. Realize God is in control of all circumstances.

2. Recognize people for what they are—people.
3. Remember your goal in life.

Doubts

1. Honestly admit you have doubts.
2. Rely upon the fellowship of other believers.
3. Remember the promises and power of God.
4. Bring your doubts directly to the Lord.

Pride

1. Be alert to the dangers of pride.
2. Be honest with yourself and God.
3. Be thankful to God for what you are in His sight.

Fear

1. Realize fear is not part of God's plan for your life.
2. Recognize you do not face your problems alone — God is with you.
3. Rest in the peace of Christ.

Death

1. View death as the steppingstone to eternity.
2. View death as a promotion.
3. Remember death has been conquered by life.